How to Get Divorced as a Stay-at-Home Parent:

The ultimate, judgment-free guide packed with scripts, checklists, self-care tools, and budget-friendly support for stay-at-home parents

Genevieve "Jenny" Dreizen

Olivia Dreizen Howell

FIRST EDITION

This book was set in 10-14 pt. Times New Roman

by Fresh Starts Registry

ISBN 979-8-9881059-9-2

Published by Fresh Starts Registry

Distributed by Fresh Starts Registry

FreshStartsRegistry.com

Please note: This book is not intended to provide legal advice or replace professional legal counsel. It is a supportive, informational guide designed to help you feel more organized, empowered, and prepared as you navigate your divorce journey. Every situation is unique, and while this workbook offers tools, checklists, and general guidance, it is not a substitute for advice from a licensed attorney or financial professional. Use this book as a companion to your process—not as a legal directive—and always consult the appropriate experts for decisions specific to your case.

Welcome, we're so glad you're here.

*We're really proud of you
for making a brave choice.*

Hey there,

Before we dive in, we want you to feel completely comfortable with this book. If the title feels too bold or you'd prefer a bit more privacy, just send us an email at hi@freshstartsregistry.com with your address, and we'll send you a discreet, no-fuss sticker to cover it up. Your comfort matters to us, always.

— The Fresh Starts Team

DEDICATION:

This book is dedicated to our Mommom, Sue Dillof—who always wanted to be a doctor, but became a mother of four instead.

She spent years as a "domestic engineer" before finding the bravery to start over. Her divorce was an act of courage. Her second act—a career as a high school biology teacher—was a declaration of independence.

She built a life on her own terms, and in doing so, showed us what strength looks like: quiet, determined, and unshakeable.

She was a stay-at-home mom who didn't have access, but found her way anyway.

Because of her, we know how to begin again. Because of her, we believe in fresh starts.

This book is for her, and for everyone who has ever dared to rewrite the story.

With love,

Olivia & Jenny

Introduction:

Let's just start here: You are not alone.

If you've picked up this book, it probably means something inside you is stirring. Maybe you've been Googling divorce in secret. Maybe you've asked a few questions in a Facebook group, then deleted the post. Maybe you've opened your notes app and written the words: I think I want a divorce.

We want you to know—we see you. We've been there. And this book is for you.

It's for the stay-at-home parent who hasn't had a paycheck in years and doesn't know how they'd even begin to afford a lawyer.

It's for the full-time caregiver who has been told they don't do anything all day but is actually holding the entire household together with invisible labor.

It's for the person who feels like they're standing at the edge of a cliff, wondering if they can leap toward freedom without falling apart.

We created this guide because the traditional divorce world wasn't built for you. It was built for people with salaries, lawyers on speed dial, and a team of experts. And while we're big fans of expert advice (we've got plenty of that in here), this isn't a book about being perfect—it's a book about surviving. About moving one step forward, and then another. About setting yourself up for your own version of success, even if you're starting with nothing.

This is not legal advice. This is survival advice.

It's the book we wish we had when we were starting over.

We're not here to tell you what to do. We're here to walk with you while you figure out what's right for you. You are not broken. You are not behind. You are not too late. You are navigating one of the hardest things a person can go through—and you're doing it without a map.

So we made one for you.

You deserve support. You deserve stability. You deserve sovereignty.

Let's begin.

With love and full belief in you,

Olivia & Jenny

CHAPTER 1

———

What Divorce Looks Like (and What It Doesn't)

Divorce isn't a one-size-fits-all event—it's a process. And when you're a stay-at-home parent with no income and little legal experience, it can feel like trying to read a map in another language. This chapter is your decoder ring. We'll walk you through the basic steps, explain what's really going on when people say "I'm filing," and introduce you to the terms and options that will show up again and again as you move forward. Don't worry—we're keeping it simple and judgment-free. You're not supposed to know all of this already. That's why we're here.

What Is Divorce, Actually?

Forget the movies. Divorce isn't about courtroom drama and sudden freedom. It's a legal process that untangles your life from someone else's: financially, logistically, and (eventually) emotionally.

When you get divorced, you and your spouse are making official decisions—either together or through the court—about things like: Custody and parenting time, child support, alimony (also called spousal support), division of property (including debt!), health insurance, where you'll each live.

You don't have to have it all figured out right now. But you do need to know: this process is made up of steps. And you can take them one at a time.

What Divorce Is Not:

Let's clear this up:

Divorce is not failure.

Divorce is not selfish.

Divorce is not a luxury for rich people.

Divorce is not always the dramatic rupture it's made out to be.

Divorce is a tool. It's a system. It's paperwork. It's a recalibration. It's a way to say, This is not working for me anymore—and I deserve better.

The Four Main Paths to Divorce

There's more than one way to get divorced—and the path you choose can depend on money, safety, communication, and state laws. Here are the four most common options:

Contested Divorce

You and your spouse do not agree on the terms (custody, money, property). This often involves court hearings and lawyers—and tends to take longer and cost more.

Uncontested Divorce

You and your spouse agree on the terms and just need to file and finalize. It's faster and usually cheaper. You can often file pro se (on your own) or use online services.

Mediated Divorce

You hire a neutral third party (a mediator) to help you come to an agreement without going to court. This can work well if you can still communicate, even if things are tense.

Collaborative Divorce

Each spouse hires a specially trained collaborative attorney, and you agree not to go to court. You work as a team with professionals (lawyers, financial advisors, therapists) to find a solution.

The Basic Divorce Timeline

Every state is different, but most divorces go something like this:

1. Filing a petition: One person officially starts the divorce by submitting paperwork to the court.

2. Serving papers: Your spouse is formally notified.

3. Response: Your spouse has a chance to agree or contest.

4. Temporary orders: In some cases, the court can make short-term decisions about custody, support, or housing.

5. Discovery + negotiation: You exchange documents and (hopefully) come to agreements.

6. Final hearing or agreement: You either sign a final agreement—or the court decides for you.

Divorce Glossary: 40 Must-Know Terms

Affidavit: A written statement you sign under oath, swearing it's true.

Alimony (Spousal Support): Money one spouse may pay the other after the divorce to help support them financially.

Arrears: Unpaid child support or alimony that is still owed.

Child Support: Money one parent pays the other to help cover the child's needs like food, clothes, and school.

Contempt of Court: When someone disobeys a court order—like ignoring a custody plan or not paying support.

Contested Divorce: When the spouses don't agree on important things like money or custody.

Custody: Decides who takes care of the kids and who makes major decisions for them.

Decree (or Judgment) of Divorce: The final document from the court saying the marriage is legally over.

Deposition: A formal interview where someone answers questions under oath before trial.

Discovery: The part of the process where both sides exchange important info like money and property details.

Dissolution of Marriage: Another legal term for divorce—it means the marriage is officially ended.

Emancipation: When a child becomes legally independent before age 18, which may end child support.

Equitable Distribution: Dividing property fairly in a divorce—but not always 50/50.

Exclusive Use: When the court lets one person live in the home or use property while the divorce is going on.

Filing Fee: The cost you pay to officially file divorce papers with the court.

Forensic Accountant: A financial expert who helps figure out complex money issues or find hidden assets.

Guardian ad Litem (Attorney for the Child): A person appointed to look out for a child's best interests in the case.

Interrogatories: A list of written questions one spouse sends the other during discovery, which must be answered truthfully.

Legal Separation: A court-approved arrangement where you're still married but live separately with rules in place.

Marital Property: Things bought or earned during the marriage—like money, cars, or homes—that may be divided.

Marital Settlement Agreement (MSA): A written agreement that covers custody, money, and property once you both agree on everything.

Mediator: A neutral person who helps both spouses come to an agreement without going to court.

Modification: A legal change to a divorce order, like changing support or custody.

No-Fault Divorce: A divorce where no one is blamed; you just say the marriage isn't working.

Order of Protection (Restraining Order): A legal order that keeps one person away from another, often for safety reasons.

Parenting Plan: A detailed schedule and set of agreements for how both parents will raise the kids after divorce.

Petition for Divorce: The official paperwork that starts the divorce process.

Pro Se: Representing yourself in court without a lawyer.

QDRO (Qualified Domestic Relations Order): A court order used to split retirement accounts between divorcing spouses.

Respondent: The person who gets served with the divorce papers and responds to them.

Retainer: Money you pay upfront to hire a lawyer.

Separate Property: Property you had before the marriage—or got as a gift or inheritance—that usually stays yours.

Settlement: An agreement between the spouses about money, kids, and property without going to trial.

Temporary Orders: Short-term rules from the court about things like who lives where or pays what while the divorce is happening.

Trial: If you can't agree, you go to court and a judge decides for you.

Uncontested Divorce: When both spouses agree on everything and just need the court to finalize it.

Visitation (Parenting Time): The plan for when the kids will spend time with the non-custodial parent.

Witness: Someone who testifies or provides evidence in your divorce case.

Withdrawal of Counsel: When a lawyer officially stops representing a client in a case.

Waiver: When one side gives up a legal right, like being formally served with papers or appearing at a hearing.

Are You Ready to Begin?

You don't need to know every legal term.

You don't need to have a full plan.

You don't need permission from anyone but yourself.

But if you're here, it means something in you is ready for more. And that's enough to begin.

Here are a few honest questions to ask yourself—not to intimidate you, but to help you gently prepare for what's next. You don't need "yes" answers to all of them. But thinking them through will help you know what to do first.

Do I know what kind of divorce I might be facing?

You don't need to pick a path yet—but do you have a general idea of whether your spouse will agree or fight? Whether you can talk or need a third party? Knowing what's likely can help you choose where to start and what kind of help to look for.

Do I have a safe place to stay during the process?

This doesn't mean you need to move tomorrow—but have you thought about your physical safety, your children's well-being, or where you'll live if you need to leave quickly? Even just identifying your options is a powerful step.

Do I have some kind of support—emotional, logistical, or financial?

You don't need a full divorce team yet. But is there someone you trust enough to tell what you're going through? Can you call in a favor, ask for a letter of support, or find a free legal consult? Your "team" can start with just one kind person who believes you.

Am I ready to take the next small step?

Not a leap. Not a sprint. Just a step. That might be reading the next chapter. Downloading a worksheet. Opening a secret email account. Calling legal aid. Telling your best friend. Small steps count. That's how real change starts.

If your answer to any of these is even a maybe, then you're not stuck—you're on your way.

You're not behind. You're not alone. And you are absolutely capable of doing this.

CHAPTER 2

———

Taking Stock of Your Life

Before you make a plan, before you file anything, you need to know where you stand. This chapter will walk you through a simple, judgment-free audit of your current situation—housing, money, kids, paperwork, health insurance, and more. Think of this as your pre-game huddle. The goal isn't to fix everything today—it's just to see everything clearly so you can start moving forward with your eyes open.

Where Are You Living, and Can You Stay There?

When people think about divorce, they often picture lawyers and courtrooms. But for stay-at-home parents, one of the most urgent and scary questions is this:

Where am I going to live?

You might be in a home you've shared with your spouse for years—or just a small rental that you've managed together. But as you begin to prepare for divorce, it's essential to take stock of your current housing situation and start thinking ahead. You don't need to move tomorrow. But knowing your options—and your limits—can help you feel more grounded and prepared for what's next.

Do You Rent or Own?

Start with the basics. Knowing whether you rent or own will determine what kind of documentation you'll need and what your options are.

Ask yourself:

- Do we rent or own this home?

- Whose name is on the lease or mortgage? Just theirs? Both of ours? Mine?

- Whose name is on the utility bills or insurance policies?

- Are we behind on any rent or mortgage payments?

If you're not sure about the answers—that's okay. Your job right now is just to gather the facts.

Are You Safe Here—Right Now?

This is about more than legal rights or who pays the bills. This is about your safety—physically, emotionally, and financially.

Ask yourself honestly:

Physically Safe:

- Do I feel physically safe living with this person?

- Do I worry that things could escalate if I bring up divorce?

- Do I have a private place to go in the house if I need space or protection?

Emotionally Safe:

- Do I feel constantly monitored, criticized, or undermined?

- Can I relax or speak freely in this environment?

- Is this a place where I can make clear-headed decisions?

Financially Safe (Short-Term):

- Can I stay here for the next few months if I need to?

- Do I have any control over the rent/mortgage payments or are they entirely in my spouse's hands?

- Is there a risk that I'll be locked out, cut off, or pressured to leave?

This isn't about jumping to conclusions. It's about paying attention to red flags and preparing options in case you need to leave sooner than planned.

If You Had to Leave—Where Would You Go?

We're not saying you will have to leave. But it's smart to think about where you might land if things shift quickly.

Ask yourself:

- Do I have a friend or family member I could stay with short-term?

- Could I apply for temporary housing or a domestic violence shelter if needed?

- Is there a hotel or safe place I could afford with short-term help?

- Do I need to start putting together a "go bag" of essentials just in case?

You might not need these things. But just knowing where your lifeboats are can make you feel calmer, clearer, and more in control.

Pro Tip: *If safety is a concern, start gathering a small folder of essential documents (IDs, health insurance cards, birth certificates, etc.) and storing them somewhere secure—either outside the home or digitally with password protection.*

This isn't about being paranoid—it's about being prepared. You deserve to feel safe in your own home. If that's not true right now, you're not overreacting. You're responding with strength.

What Money Do You Actually Have Access To?

Let's be honest—money is one of the scariest parts of getting divorced, especially when you're a stay-at-home parent who hasn't earned income in a while (or ever). And when your partner has been the one handling the finances, you might feel like you're staring into a locked vault.

But here's the truth: you don't need to know everything. You just need to start finding out what you can.

This section is about gathering information—not assigning blame, not making big moves, and definitely not panicking. The more you know now, the better you'll be able to plan.

Do You Have Access to Any Accounts?

This is your first major question. It doesn't matter if your name is on the account—can you actually see it?

Ask yourself:

- Do I know what bank(s) we use?

- Can I log in online to view our checking or savings account?

- Do I have access to a credit card (and is it in my name or shared)?

- Do I have a personal checking/savings account?

- Do I get paper statements, or does everything go to my spouse's email?

If the answer to most of these is no, you're not alone—and you're not stuck. But this is your sign to start writing down whatever scraps of info you can find.

Pro Tip: *If you've ever used online banking (even years ago), check your browser history or old emails for login info or alerts. Every bit of access helps.*

What Money Do You Actually Have Access To?

Let's be honest—money is one of the scariest parts of getting divorced, especially when you're a stay-at-home parent who hasn't earned income in a while (or ever). And when your partner has been the one handling the finances, you might feel like you're staring into a locked vault.

But here's the truth: you don't need to know everything. You just need to start finding out what you can.

This section is about gathering information—not assigning blame, not making big moves, and definitely not panicking. The more you know now, the better you'll be able to plan.

Do You Have Access to Any Accounts?

This is your first major question. It doesn't matter if your name is on the account—can you actually see it?

Ask yourself:

- Do I know what bank(s) we use?

- Can I log in online to view our checking or savings account?

- Do I have access to a credit card (and is it in my name or shared)?

- Do I have a personal checking/savings account?

- Do I get paper statements, or does everything go to my spouse's email?

If the answer to most of these is no, you're not alone—and you're not stuck. But this is your sign to start writing down whatever scraps of info you can find.

Pro Tip: *If you've ever used online banking (even years ago), check your browser history or old emails for login info or alerts. Every bit of access helps.*

What Comes In—and What Goes Out?

You don't need a perfect spreadsheet, but it helps to get a rough sense of the household flow.

Try to answer:

- What is my partner's monthly income? (Estimate if you don't know exactly.)

- Are there any recurring payments I know of? (Mortgage, rent, car, childcare?)

- Do we receive any benefits (SNAP, child tax credit, unemployment, SSI)?

- Do we owe any debts or have any loans?

- Do I have any personal income—even small or irregular amounts?

Start a list. Don't worry about being perfect—this is your Financial Clarity Draft, Not Final. Use the What Comes In—and What Goes Out? Worksheet to begin this process.

What Comes In—and What Goes Out?

Your Financial Clarity Draft (Not Final!)

This is a starting place—not a final spreadsheet. Just get it out of your head and onto the page.

INCOME

1. What is my partner's monthly income?

Estimated amount: _____ (Estimate if unsure)

Notes (source, job, etc): _____

_____

2. Do I receive any benefits?

 Check all that apply:

☐ SNAP   ☐ SSI

☐ Child Tax Credit   ☐ Other: _____

☐ Unemployment

Total monthly benefits: _____

3. Do I have any personal income (big or small)?

Side jobs, freelance work, gifts, anything you bring in:

Amount: _____

Notes: _____

_____

_____

What Comes In—and What Goes Out? (cont.)

EXPENSES: What recurring payments do I know of? List everything you can think of—don't worry if it's not exact.

Expense Type	Monthly Amount	In Whose Name?	Notes
Rent/Mortgage			
Utilities (Gas/ Electric/Water)			
Car Payment			
Car Insurance			
Childcare/School			
Groceries			
Cell Phones			
Subscriptions			
Credit Cards			
Other			

DEBTS & LOANS: Do we owe any debts or have loans? List credit cards, student loans, car loans, personal loans, medical debt, etc.

Debt Type	Balance Owed	Monthly Payments	In Whose Name?

What Comes In—and What Goes Out? (cont.)

MONEY ACCESS CHECKLIST

Questions	Yes / No / Unsure	Notes
Do I know where our money is kept? (Bank accounts, Venmo, PayPal, etc.)		
Do I have access to these accounts?		
Do I have my own account?		
Do I have login info for shared accounts?		
Do I receive paper statements or emails?		
Are there accounts or assets I suspect exist but don't know details about?		
Do I need help accessing anything?		

If You Don't Have Access—What Can You Do?

It's common in long-term relationships for one person to control the finances. But you still have the right to know what's going on with money that affects you and your children.

Here's what you can start doing:

Ask your bank for a printed statement.

If you share an account, you're entitled to request info at your local branch.

Start collecting mail.

Keep an eye out for bank statements, loan notices, or bills. Take photos or store copies in a safe place.

Call a legal aid clinic (more on this in Chapter 3)

You may be able to request financial disclosure from your spouse later on through the divorce process—but getting even a partial picture now can help you prepare. More on this later!

Open a bank account in your name only (more on this in Chapter 11)

Use a trusted institution (online or local). Most require just a photo ID and a small opening balance (some are free with $0).

Sample Script: "Hi, I'm trying to open a checking account in my name only. I don't currently have access to shared funds. Can you help me understand what I need to do?"

Pro Tip: *You don't have to tell your spouse you're doing this—especially if you're worried about retaliation. Your financial safety comes first.*

What If You Don't Have Any Money?

Take a breath. You are not alone. And this is not the end of your story.

- ○ Here's what you can do:

- ○ Apply for emergency assistance (more in Chapter 7)

- ○ Ask a trusted friend or family member for a small stopgap loan (we'll help with scripts in Chapter 4)

- ○ Look into "In Forma Pauperis" court waivers (Chapter 3)

- ○ Start a tiny savings stash—even $5 at a time

What Are Your Parenting Responsibilities?

Let's be honest: if you're a stay-at-home parent, you've probably been doing a lot—without pay, without recognition, and often without support. And while you may just think of it as "being a parent," the truth is: what you've been doing is work.

This section will help you map out the invisible labor you've been handling every day—because later in the divorce process, you may need to explain it to a judge, a lawyer, or even your co-parent. More importantly, you need to see it too. This is part of your power.

What Does a Day in Your Parenting Life Look Like?

Start with the daily basics:

- Who wakes the kids up and gets them ready?

- Who packs lunches and handles school drop-off and pick-up?

- Who handles naptime, screen time, bedtime routines?

- Who takes care of clothing, laundry, hygiene, and meals?

You don't need to have done everything to be the primary parent. But if you've been the one holding the rhythm of the home, it matters. A lot.

Who Handles the Emotional + Logistical Load?

This is the "stuff" no one sees but that makes the household function:

- Scheduling doctor and dentist appointments

- Managing school calendars, permission slips, and school projects

- Packing bags for daycare, aftercare, playdates

- Buying birthday gifts, sending RSVPs, remembering allergies

- Noticing when the kids are sick, sad, overstimulated, or struggling

- Managing sibling dynamics, discipline, emotional meltdowns

These tasks don't show up on paper—but they build the emotional safety net for your children.

Reminder: *Courts often look at who has historically provided the majority of care when determining custody arrangements. That includes emotional caregiving—not just logistics.*

What About Your Spouse's Role?

This isn't about bashing anyone—it's about getting real.

Ask yourself:

- Does your partner help with school drop-off or bedtime?

- Do they take the kids to appointments or stay home when they're sick?

- Do they know your child's teacher's name? Their shoe size?

- Could they step into your daily role seamlessly, or would they be lost?

You don't have to write this down for them—but you should write it down for yourself. If you ever need to prove that you've been the primary caregiver, these details matter.

Do You Have Help from Others?

Even if you're the main caregiver, you might have help. Let's map that out too:

- Grandparents or extended family

- Babysitters or nannies

- After-school programs

- Co-ops, religious groups, or neighbor support

This support system counts—but it also reinforces the fact that you're the one coordinating all of it.

Use the Caregiving Breakdown Worksheet to:

Track daily parenting responsibilities

- List medical, school, and emotional caregiving roles

- Record your spouse's contributions (or lack thereof)

- Identify your existing support network for parenting

Why This Matters

You've probably been told, implicitly or explicitly, that this work isn't "real" work. But in the eyes of the law—and in the real world—it is.

When it comes time to talk about custody, visitation, or parenting plans, you need to be able to show what you do. Not because you have to prove you're a good parent (you already are), but because this is about advocating for your role and your kids' stability.

You're not "just" a parent. You've been doing the job of a full-time case manager, therapist, chef, chauffeur, advocate, and emotional anchor. Now you get to claim that truth out loud.

What Paperwork Do You Already Have?

Let's get one thing out of the way: you do not need to become a legal filing cabinet overnight. But when you're preparing for divorce—especially if your spouse has handled most of the household finances—it's crucial to begin collecting and organizing important documents now, before anything gets messy, restricted, or erased.

You may not need all of this paperwork right away. But the earlier you have it, the more empowered and protected you'll be—especially if things become contentious.

Start With What You Know (and Can Find)

Don't panic if you don't know where the tax returns are or what bank you even use. Start small and close to home. Open drawers. Scroll through your inbox. Check the glove compartment.

Here's a list of priority documents to begin looking for:

Identity & Vital Records:

- Your photo ID (driver's license or state ID)

- Social Security cards (yours and your kids')

- Marriage certificate

- Kids' birth certificates

- Passports

Financial Records:

- Bank statements (checking, savings, credit union)
- Credit card statements
- Tax returns (last 2–3 years, personal and joint)
- Pay stubs or proof of income (yours and/or your spouse's)
- Loan documents (auto, student, personal)

Housing Documents:

- Lease agreement or mortgage documents
- Utility bills (proof of address)
- Property tax records (if applicable)
- Insurance policies (home/renters)

Healthcare & Insurance:

- Health insurance cards and policies
- Medical bills and receipts
- List of medications and providers
- Life insurance policies

Legal & Custody:

- Prenuptial or postnuptial agreements (if they exist)
- Existing custody or court agreements (if applicable)
- Restraining orders or safety documents (if applicable)
- Court notices, legal correspondence

Start a Safe, Private Storage System

You'll need a place to keep what you're collecting—ideally somewhere your spouse can't access. Some ideas:

- A password-protected Google Drive or Dropbox folder
- A portable file box that stays with a trusted friend
- A USB flash drive with important scans
- A locked cabinet, drawer, or safe (if you're still living together)

Safety Tip: *If you're using a shared computer or email, create a new private account for divorce-related documents and communication. Use an incognito browser when needed.*

Find the Experts you need at freshstartsregistry.com/experts

Caregiving Breakdown Worksheet

Your Daily Parenting Responsibilities—Made Visible. You've been doing the work. Let's make sure it's seen.

A Day in Your Parenting Life: Who does the following tasks most often? Write in "M" for "Me," "T" for "Them," and "B" for "Both."

Task	Who handles	Notes
Wake kids up & get them ready		
Make breakfast		
Pack lunches		
School/daycare drop-off		
Naptime or rest time		
Screen time setup/supervision		
Dinner prep and clean-up		
Bath time & hygiene		
Bedtime routine		
Middle-of-the-night care		

Who Carries the Emotional + Logistical Load? Write in "M" for "Me," "T" for "Them," and "B" for "Both."

Task	Who handles	Notes
Schedule doctor/dentist appointments		
Keep track of vaccines, medications, allergies		
Monitor symptoms and emotional well-being		
Plan meals, manage grocery list, prep food		
Handle school emails, calendars, permission slips		
Know teachers' names, friends' names, routines		
Manage playdates, RSVPs, birthday gifts		
Help with homework and school projects		
Coordinate extracurriculars (lessons, sports, etc.)		
Address discipline, meltdowns, and emotional needs		
Track and replace clothing, shoes, supplies		

Notes:

_____

_____

_____

_____

Your Partner's Parenting Role: Write honestly and clearly.

What do they consistently help with?

_____

_____

_____

Do they know important info (doctor, teacher, schedule)?

_____

_____

_____

Could they take over your routine if needed? Why or why not?

_____

_____

_____

When the kids are sick, who stays home or arranges care?

_____

_____

_____

Outside Help & Support Network: List who helps and how. This reinforces your central role in coordinating care.

Person/Program	Role (Babysitter, Grandma, etc.)	Frequency/Details

Final Reflection (Optional) How do you feel reading this back to yourself?

What do you want a lawyer, judge, or mediator to understand about your parenting?

_____

_____

_____

_____

_____

_____

_____

This isn't just about custody—it's about recognizing the care work you've been doing every day, often without acknowledgment. You don't need to be perfect. You just need to be honest.

Document Checklist for Divorce Prep

Start With What You Know (and Can Find)

Use this checklist to track what you've found, what's missing, and where things are stored (physically or digitally). Progress is progress—even one document at a time.

Personal Identification & Vital Records

- ☐ Photo ID (driver's license, passport)

- ☐ Social Security cards (yours and your children's)

- ☐ Marriage certificate

- ☐ Birth certificates (for you, your spouse, and children)

- ☐ Immigration documents (if applicable)

- ☐ Passports

Financial Records

- ☐ Recent pay stubs (yours and your spouse's)

- ☐ Tax returns (past 2–3 years, personal and joint)

- ☐ Bank statements (checking, savings, credit union accounts)

- ☐ Retirement account statements (401(k), IRA, pension plans)

- ☐ Investment account statements (stocks, bonds, crypto, etc.)

- ☐ Credit card statements (individual and joint)

- ☐ Loan documents (mortgage, student, auto, personal)

- ☐ List of all debts and liabilities

- ☐ Proof of assets (valuable possessions, collectibles, etc.)

Document Checklist for Divorce Prep (cont.)

Housing & Property Records

- ☐ Lease agreement or mortgage documents

- ☐ Property deed(s)

- ☐ Property tax statements

- ☐ Utility bills (proof of residence or to establish living arrangements)

- ☐ Home appraisal or market analysis (if available)

- ☐ Insurance & Healthcare

Health insurance policy documents

- ☐ Life insurance policies (individual and employer-provided)

- ☐ Auto and home/renters insurance documents

- ☐ List of current prescriptions and healthcare providers

- ☐ Medical bills and expenses

Legal Documents

- ☐ Prenuptial or postnuptial agreements (if applicable)

- ☐ Previous court orders or judgments (including from other cases)

- ☐ Custody or parenting agreements (formal or informal)

- ☐ Protective or restraining orders

- ☐ Documentation of any abuse or unsafe situations (photos, messages, police reports)

If You Can't Access Something—Make a Note

Sometimes paperwork is missing because your spouse has full control. That's incredibly common—and doesn't mean you're out of options.

Write down everything you know exists, even if you can't get it yet.

Ex: "Spouse's 401(k) at Fidelity." "Tax returns filed jointly 2021–2023."

Later on, a lawyer or legal aid clinic can help request official copies. But your memory and observations are valuable.

Sample Note: "Joint bank account at Chase, accessed via spouse's phone only. I've seen statements arrive monthly. Not sure of account number."

ProTip: Keep a Missing-but-Important Tracker. Keep track of the documents you know are out there but can't currently access, so you don't lose sight of them later.

Build This Slowly and Quietly

You don't have to collect every form in one weekend. You're building your independence brick by brick. Set a timer for 10 minutes. That's it. Open one drawer. Snap one photo. Write down one account name. Little by little, it adds up—and it matters.

Healthcare and Insurance: What's in Place—and What Happens Next?

If you've been on your spouse's health insurance, the idea of divorce might bring up one very real and terrifying question:

"What happens if I lose coverage?"

Health insurance can feel like a luxury when you've been financially dependent, but in divorce, it's a non-negotiable lifeline—for you and your kids. This section will help you understand what you're currently covered by, what might happen to that coverage in divorce, and what your options are if you suddenly find yourself uninsured.

What's Your Current Coverage?

Start with what you know. Don't worry if you don't have the full policy in hand—just write down what you do know.

Ask yourself:

- Am I covered under my spouse's employer plan?
- Are my children also covered under that plan?
- Do I have my own policy, or am I uninsured?
- What's the name of the insurance provider?
- Have I used it recently (doctor visits, prescriptions, dental)?
- Have I seen ID cards or explanation of benefits statements?

Pro Tip: Look for emails, cards in your wallet, paperwork from pediatricians or pharmacies. Clues can come from anywhere.

What Happens to Insurance During Divorce?

Here's the typical process in most U.S. divorces:

If you're on your spouse's insurance, you'll remain covered until the divorce is finalized.

After the divorce is complete, you'll likely lose access to their employer-provided plan. (Some plans may offer COBRA continuation, but it's expensive.)

Children may remain on either parent's policy, depending on the court's custody and support agreements.

That means you need to start exploring your own options early, so there's no lapse in coverage.

What Are Your Options If You Lose Coverage?

You're not without options—even if you have $0 coming in right now. Here's where to look:

1. Medicaid

- Free or low-cost health coverage for low-income adults and children.
- Available in most states with a simple online application.
- Covers doctor visits, prescriptions, hospital stays, and more.

2. CHIP (Children's Health Insurance Program)

- Covers kids in families that earn too much for Medicaid but still need help.
- Often used for dental, vision, and pediatric needs.

3. ACA Marketplace (Healthcare.gov)

- You may qualify for $0 or low-cost plans if your income is limited.
- Losing coverage due to divorce counts as a qualifying life event, meaning you can apply outside of the open enrollment window.

4. COBRA (Not ideal, but worth mentioning)

- Lets you stay on your ex's plan temporarily—but you pay the full premium.
- Often too expensive if you have no income, but can be a short-term backup.

What About Medications and Medical Needs Right Now?

If you or your kids have current prescriptions, therapy sessions, or upcoming appointments, don't wait to plan.

Ask:

- Do I have upcoming medical or dental appointments?
- Do I need to refill any prescriptions soon?
- Is there a mental health provider I rely on?
- Do I need to get copies of medical records for my kids or myself?

Pro Tip: Ask your pharmacy for a printout of past prescriptions—it may help establish medical needs and continuity of care during custody discussions.

What to Gather Now

Even if you're not planning to make a change yet, start gathering:

- Copies of insurance cards
- Policy numbers and provider phone numbers
- A list of your current providers and medications
- Login info for any online portals
- Receipts or statements from recent visits (if available)

What If You've Gone Without Coverage?

First of all, no shame. Millions of people live without coverage in the U.S.—especially stay-at-home parents. But divorce is a good time to take steps to get re-covered, even temporarily.

You can apply for Medicaid, the ACA Marketplace, or local assistance through your county health department or community health centers.

Most states **consider divorce or legal separation a "qualifying life event,"** which means you don't have to wait for the usual enrollment period to apply.

What About Mental Health Support?

Mental health care is health care. Whether you're trying to survive the chaos or get help for your kids, therapy can be a lifeline.

Even if you don't have insurance right now, you may be able to:

- Access sliding-scale or free therapy through local clinics or nonprofits
- Use online therapy platforms with low-income discounts
- Find therapists offering low-cost services for divorce support groups

Find the Experts you need at freshstartsregistry.com/experts

Healthcare is not a luxury. It's not selfish. It's not optional.

Your health and your children's health are foundational to your safety and your future—and we want you to have a plan in place, even if it's imperfect.

Let's be real—going through a divorce as a stay-at-home parent can feel isolating. You might not have coworkers to vent to. You may feel like your whole world is wrapped around your kids. And maybe, just maybe, you've been pretending everything's fine for so long that no one even knows you're struggling.

What Kind of Support System Do You Have?

We want to stop you right here and say: you don't have to do this alone.

Even if your support system feels nonexistent right now, this section will help you see what's already around you—and how to start building what you need from scratch.

First, Take Inventory of What You Do Have

Let's get honest—not hopeless.

Ask yourself:

- Is there anyone in your life who knows what's going on?

- (A friend, sibling, neighbor, Facebook friend you trust?)

- Who would take your kids in an emergency?

- Who would loan you $50 if you asked?

- Who would sit with you in court if you needed them to?

Even one "yes" is a building block.

Next, Learn to Make the Ask

Here's the hard truth: people don't know how to show up unless you ask. That doesn't mean you have to explain everything, overshare, or perform your pain—but it does mean getting brave enough to say:

"I'm going through a divorce, and I'm having a really hard time. Can you check in on me once a week via text?"

"I may need help watching the kids during a court appointment—can I ask you when the time comes?"

"Would you be willing to go with me to open a bank account?"

"Can I just vent to you for five minutes without advice?"

Use our Soft Ask Script Bank in Chapter 4 if asking feels too scary right now.

Remember: the people who love you want to help. Sometimes they just need permission.

Finding Support Online + In Your Community

If you don't have strong connections IRL, that's okay. There are so many ways to build support—even quietly and digitally.

Start here:

Local resources

Libraries, women's centers, domestic violence shelters (even if your situation isn't abusive), food pantries, community orgs

Online communities

Facebook groups for single moms, divorce support, or even local buy/sell/trade groups where resources circulate, reach out to @freshstartsregistry on social media and we'll connect you with resources!

Faith groups

If you're religious or spiritual, churches, mosques, and synagogues often offer practical help with no strings attached

School-based support

Many school social workers or parent liaisons can help you access resources (and they are not mandated to tell your spouse)

Check In with Yourself

Support isn't just who you know—it's also how you're holding up.

Ask yourself:

- Am I getting any rest?

- Am I feeding myself (even if it's toast)?

- Am I being kind to my nervous system?

- Am I giving myself permission to feel scared, messy, or numb?

You don't have to "bounce back." You just have to keep showing up. Let support be receiving, not performing.

CHAPTER 3

Free and Low-Cost Legal Help

Hiring a lawyer sounds expensive because... it usually is. But here's what no one tells you: there are free and affordable legal options out there, and many stay-at-home parents use them every single day. You do not have to wait until you can afford a big retainer to start the divorce process. This chapter walks you through every no-cost and low-cost resource available to help you move forward—even if you have $0 in your bank account.

Where to Find Free or Affordable Legal Support

Let's bust a myth right now: you don't need to spend $20,000 to get divorced. You do need clarity, information, and access. Fortunately, there are resources specifically built for people just like you—people who've done unpaid labor for years and are now trying to reclaim their independence.

Legal Aid and Sliding Scale Legal Services

What is Legal Aid?

Legal Aid is free or low-cost legal assistance provided by nonprofit organizations. These services are typically reserved for people who meet certain income eligibility guidelines, and they often focus on critical issues like family law (divorce, custody, child support), housing, domestic violence, public benefits, and immigration.

Legal Aid organizations are funded through federal, state, local, and private grants, and their goal is simple: to ensure everyone has access to legal representation, regardless of income.

Where to Find It: Visit LSC.gov (Legal Services Corporation) to find free legal aid programs near you.

What Are Sliding Scale Legal Services?

Sliding Scale Legal Services (sometimes called "low bono" services) are provided by private attorneys or law firms who adjust their fees based on your income and financial situation. Instead of charging standard hourly rates, they offer a flexible pricing structure, so the cost fits your budget.

Where to Find It: Search local law firms, bar association directories, or ask directly if an attorney offers "sliding scale" or "low bono" options.

Why This Is a Smart Move

Professional Representation Matters:

Even if you're resourceful and independent, divorce, custody battles, or property division are high-stakes legal matters. Proper advice and representation can prevent long-term financial and emotional fallout.

Affordability:

Instead of draining savings or going into debt, you can access the legal expertise you need — either for free or for a manageable cost.

Critical for High-Conflict Situations:

If your divorce or legal matter involves children, allegations of abuse, or significant assets, having a lawyer isn't just helpful — it's essential to protect your rights and future.

How to Access Legal Aid or Sliding Scale Services

Here's a clear, simple action plan you can follow:

Step 1: Find Legal Aid Near You

Go to LSC.gov.

Click "Find Legal Aid."

Enter your state or zip code to see local legal aid organizations.

Check eligibility requirements (each organization may vary slightly).

Step 2: Contact Your Local Courthouse

Many courthouses keep a list of trusted legal aid programs and sliding scale attorneys. They can often refer you to nonprofit groups, self-help centers, or bar association programs.

Phone Script for Calling Your Local Courthouse:

"Hi, my name is [Your Name]. I'm looking for free or low-cost legal help for [brief description of your issue, e.g., a divorce or custody matter]. Could you please direct me to any legal aid organizations or sliding scale attorneys in our area?"

[If they say they have referrals:]

"Thank you so much! Is there an email address or website where I can also find more information?"

Step 3: Search for Sliding Scale or "Low Bono" Attorneys

Use Google or your local bar association directory.

Review their websites for mentions of flexible pricing or call their office directly.

Search terms like:

"Sliding scale divorce attorney [Your City/State]"

"Low bono lawyer [Your City/State]"

"Affordable family law attorney [Your City/State]"

Phone Script for Contacting a Law Office:

"Hi, my name is [Your Name]. I'm seeking legal help for [brief description: divorce, custody, domestic violence, etc.]. Do you offer sliding scale or low bono services? If not, could you recommend someone who does?"

[If they offer it:]

"That's wonderful! Could you please share what the intake process looks like and any paperwork I should bring to a consultation?"

Step 4: Prepare Your Documents

Whether you're working with legal aid or a sliding scale attorney, you'll likely need to provide:

- Proof of income (pay stubs, tax returns, benefits statements)

- Identification (driver's license, passport, etc.)

- Documentation related to your legal issue (marriage certificate, lease agreement, protective orders, custody papers, etc.)

- Organizing these ahead of time will make the intake process smoother and faster.

Email Template for Reaching Out to Legal Aid

Subject: Request for Legal Aid Services

Hi [Organization Name],

My name is [Your Name], and I'm reaching out to inquire about free or low-cost legal assistance. I am currently seeking help with [briefly state issues: e.g., a divorce, custody arrangement, domestic violence matter]. I would appreciate any information you could share about eligibility requirements and the next steps to apply for your services.

Thank you for your time and support.

Sincerely,

[Your Name]

[Phone Number]

Extra Tips for Success

- Act Quickly: Legal aid organizations can have waitlists — call or apply as soon as you can.

- Be Honest About Your Situation: They're here to help, not judge.

- Ask About Other Resources: Many legal aid offices offer classes, workshops, and self-help materials even if they can't take your case directly.

- Stay Organized: Keep a folder (physical or digital) with all correspondence, forms, and legal documents.

- Follow Up: If you haven't heard back within a few days, it's okay to politely follow up with a call or email.

Pro Bono Attorneys:

What Is a Pro Bono Attorney?

"Pro bono" is short for pro bono publico, meaning "for the public good." Pro bono attorneys volunteer their time and legal expertise to individuals who can't afford representation—particularly survivors of abuse, people experiencing financial hardship, or those navigating major life transitions like divorce or custody disputes.

Why Seeking a Pro Bono Lawyer Is a Smart Move:

- You gain professional legal guidance from someone trained in family law

- You don't carry the burden of high legal fees

- You're not alone in navigating complex and emotional legal systems

- If your case involves domestic violence, child custody, or major financial need, you may qualify for a volunteer attorney who will represent you for free.

How to Find Pro Bono Legal Help

Here's a step-by-step guide—with scripts—to help you reach out with confidence.

Step 1: Call Your State's Bar Association

Every state has a Bar Association with a legal referral service or a pro bono program. Just Google "[Your State] Bar Association."

Phone Script:

"Hi, my name is [Your Name], and I'm looking for help with a family court issue. I can't afford a lawyer right now—do you offer any referrals to pro bono attorneys or low-cost legal services in my area?"

If they ask for more details: "I'm dealing with a [divorce / custody case / protective order], and I'd really appreciate any resources or referrals you can offer, especially someone with experience in family law."

Step 2: Contact Local Legal Aid Organizations or Clinics

Legal aid clinics often partner with pro bono lawyers or offer sliding-scale services.

Search "[Your City] legal aid family law" or try your local courthouse self-help center—they often have flyers or referrals available.

Bonus Tip: If you're a survivor of domestic violence or emotional abuse, shelters and crisis centers often work directly with pro bono attorneys and can help expedite referrals.

Step 3: Use Online Tools Like ProBono.net

Head to ProBono.net and click on your state to view resources for free or low-cost legal help. You'll find local organizations, legal clinics, and intake forms to request assistance.

What to Say When You Reach Out

Whether you're walking into a clinic or calling an agency, here's a script to guide you:

"Hi, I'm looking for legal help for a family law matter, but I can't afford to hire a private attorney. Do you have any pro bono lawyers available, or can you refer me to someone who might be able to help?"

What If I'm Nervous to Ask?

You're not alone. This process can feel intimidating—but remember: the courts are there to serve the public. You have the right to access justice, and fee waivers exist for a reason.

Here's a reminder script if you're feeling unsure:

"Hi, I'm trying to navigate this as best I can, and I'm just hoping to get some guidance. I want to file but truly can't afford the fees right now. Can you help me understand the next steps?"

Documents to Have Ready

- When applying for pro bono assistance, you may need to show proof of income or your legal situation. Have the following on hand:

- Government-issued ID

- Recent pay stubs or unemployment verification

- Any court documents related to your case

- A brief written summary of your situation (optional, but helpful)

What if I'm turned away?

Don't be discouraged—sometimes there's a waitlist or limited availability. Keep calling, keep checking in, and ask:

"Are there any upcoming legal clinics or other resources you recommend?"

Persistence pays off—and your safety and rights matter. Divorce, custody battles, and other family court issues can feel isolating—but there is help out there, even if you can't afford it. Pro bono attorneys exist for you—to make sure everyone has access to justice, regardless of income. You are not alone, and you don't have to navigate this system without support.

Free Legal Help for Divorce: How to Access Law School Legal Clinics

If you're going through a divorce, navigating a custody arrangement, or need help with family court paperwork—but can't afford a lawyer—there's a powerful, underused resource you need to know about: family law clinics at law schools.

These clinics are staffed by law students who work under the supervision of licensed attorneys, and they often offer free legal support to individuals facing financial hardship or legal challenges.

Whether you need help filing for divorce, organizing custody paperwork, or understanding your rights in family court, a legal clinic might be the perfect place to start.

What Is a Law School Legal Clinic?

A legal clinic is a program within a law school where students, under close supervision from experienced attorneys, represent real clients in real cases—at no cost to the client.

Family law clinics may assist with:

- Divorce and separation

- Custody and visitation

- Child support issues

- Domestic violence protection orders

- Court filings and procedures

Why This Is a Smart Move

- Free legal assistance from students supervised by attorneys

- You get professional-level help with your case

- Clinics are eager to help and often take on complex or low-income cases

- They work closely and thoroughly—because your case is their classroom

It's a win-win: you get legal support, and students gain real-world experience.

How to Find a Legal Clinic Near You

Step 1: Search Online

Use search terms like:

"Family law clinic [Your State] law school"

"Free divorce help [Your City] law school clinic"

"Legal aid clinic [State or City] law school"

Examples:

Boston University Family Law Clinic

University of Michigan Legal Services Clinic

Columbia Law School Lawyering in the Digital Age Clinic

UC Hastings Legal Clinics

Step 2: Reach Out Directly

Most clinics have a phone number or email for intake inquiries. Here's what to say:

Phone Script: Calling a Law School Legal Clinic

You: "Hi, my name is [Your Name], and I'm looking for free legal help with a family law issue. I saw your clinic online and wanted to ask if you're currently accepting new clients or could refer me to someone who might help."

If asked for details: "I'm going through a [divorce / custody arrangement / family court issue], and I can't afford an attorney. I'd really appreciate any guidance or support your clinic might be able to offer."

Email Template: Reaching Out to a Clinic

Subject: Seeking Family Law Assistance

Dear [Clinic Name] Team,

My name is [Your Name], and I'm looking for legal support for a [briefly explain issue—divorce, custody, etc.]. I'm currently unable to afford private legal representation and came across your clinic while researching options. Could you let me know if you're accepting new clients at this time, or if there is an intake form I should complete? I'd be grateful for any support or direction you can offer.

Thank you so much for your time and the important work you do.

Warmly,

[Your Name], [Phone Number] (optional)

What to Expect & Prepare

Each clinic operates a little differently, but many work in semester cycles and may have an application process or intake period. You may be asked to provide:

- A summary of your legal issue

- Financial information or proof of low income

- Court documents or timelines if you've already filed

- Your availability for meetings

If your case is accepted, you'll be assigned a law student (or team of students) who will represent you under attorney supervision.

Real Talk: Is This "Real" Legal Help?

Absolutely. These students are highly motivated, closely supervised, and committed to helping you succeed. Many clinics are run by professors who are respected attorneys in family law. You're not a practice case—you're a real person, and they'll treat your case with real care.

And unlike some rushed legal services, clinics often have more time and attention to give each client, because they're there to learn and serve.

Quick Action Steps

- Search online for nearby law school clinics

- Make a list of 2–3 clinics to contact

- Call or email using the scripts above

- Ask about timelines—some clinics accept clients on a rolling basis, others only per semester

- Follow up if you don't hear back within 7–10 days

Legal help doesn't have to come with a massive price tag. Law school clinics offer free, respectful, and often life-changing support for people going through some of life's hardest transitions. Whether you're trying to file for divorce, figure out custody, or just understand your legal rights—you don't have to do it alone. Reach out, ask the question, and take that first step.

You deserve support. You deserve clarity. And this resource could be the beginning of your fresh start.

One of the most underutilized tools available to you? Courthouse Self-Help Centers

When you're facing a divorce and don't have the money to hire a lawyer, it can feel like the system isn't built for you. But here's the truth: you're not alone, and there are free resources designed to help you navigate this process without breaking the bank.

What Are Self-Help Centers?

Self-help centers are typically located inside or alongside family courthouses. Many counties and states also host them online. They're designed specifically to help people like you — individuals who are filing for divorce on their own, also called "pro se" filers (that just means you don't have an attorney).

These centers offer:

- Free legal forms for divorce, custody, and support

- Step-by-step instructions

- Walk-in support (in some locations)

- Free workshops and clinics

- Staff who can answer basic questions about court process

They won't give you legal advice (they're not your lawyer), but they will help you figure out what to file, how to fill it out, and where to submit it. That's a huge deal if you're overwhelmed and under-resourced.

How Do You Find One?

Call your local family courthouse and ask: "Do you have a self-help center for family law or divorce?"

Or check their website — many states have statewide legal aid portals or court websites with links to local self-help resources.

Tip: Search "[Your County] family court self-help divorce" and you might find an entire page of free forms and instructions tailored to your situation.

Why Does This Matter?

Because divorce shouldn't be reserved for people who can afford a lawyer.

Self-help centers are one of the most powerful tools we have for making divorce more accessible, equitable, and doable — even if you have zero dollars to spare.

How to File for Divorce When You Can't Afford the Fees: Understanding Court Fee Waivers (In Forma Pauperis)

Filing for divorce—or any family court action—can be overwhelming enough without the added stress of high court filing fees. The good news? You might not have to pay them at all.

If you're struggling financially, your local courthouse may allow you to file "In Forma Pauperis"—a legal term that simply means "in the form of a pauper" or, more plainly, you can't afford the costs and need them waived. Here's everything you need to know, including exact scripts for calling your courthouse, and step-by-step instructions to get started.

What is an "In Forma Pauperis" Fee Waiver?

When you file a petition for divorce, custody, or other legal action, courts often charge filing fees that can range from $100 to $500 or more. If you're unable to pay, you can apply for a fee waiver so you're not blocked from accessing the legal system.

These waivers can cover:

- Divorce petitions
- Custody filings
- Motions and modifications
- Service fees in some cases

Why Filing for an In Forma Pauperis Waiver Is a Smart Move:

- You deserve access to the court system, no matter your financial situation.
- Saves you hundreds of dollars in up-front court costs
- Allows you to move forward with your legal process without delay
- Protects your legal rights, even during financial hardship

How to Apply for a Fee Waiver:

Step 1: Call or Visit Your Local Courthouse

You can usually find the number for your county courthouse by searching "[Your County] family court clerk."

Once you call, here's what to say: Phone Script: Asking for a Fee Waiver

"In Forma Pauperis" is pronounced: in FOR-muh PAW-puh-riss

(You might also hear it pronounced as PAW-per-iss depending on the region.)

Phone script: "Hi, my name is [Your Name], and I'm hoping to file for [divorce / custody / a family court matter], but I can't afford the court fees. Can you tell me how to apply for a fee waiver or In Forma Pauperis status?"

If redirected or given more info: "Thank you so much—I just want to make sure I do everything correctly. Is there a form I can pick up in person, or can I download it online? And what documents do I need to bring when I submit it?"

Step 2: Ask for the "In Forma Pauperis" Form

Most court clerks will know what this is. You can say: "Can you please provide the In Forma Pauperis application or fee waiver form for family court filings?"

You can often find and download the form from your court's website under "Self-Help" or "Family Law Forms."

Find the Experts you need at freshstartsregistry.com/experts

Step 3: Gather Supporting Documents

- ◦ To show financial hardship, you may need:

- ◦ Recent pay stubs (if employed)

- ◦ Unemployment documentation

- ◦ Public assistance award letters (SNAP, TANF, etc.)

- ◦ A signed affidavit of income and expenses

Step 4: Submit the Application

Return the form along with your documentation to the courthouse. In some states, a judge may need to review and sign off on your request. You may be notified by mail, or you might be asked to come in for a short hearing.

What If I'm Nervous to Ask?

You're not alone. This process can feel intimidating—but remember: the courts are there to serve the public. You have the right to access justice, and fee waivers exist for a reason.

Here's a reminder script if you're feeling unsure: "Hi, I'm trying to navigate this as best I can, and I'm just hoping to get some guidance. I want to file but truly can't afford the fees right now. Can you help me understand the next steps?"

Helpful Tips for filing an In Forma Pauperis application

- ▪ Keep copies of everything you submit

- ▪ If you're denied, ask the clerk what other options are available

- ▪ Some states offer legal aid volunteers or clinics to help with the form

- ▪ Don't be afraid to follow up if you don't hear back within a week or two

If you're feeling lost or overwhelmed, start with a single call. Ask the question. Take the next small step. You've got this. Divorce happens, but you are not alone.

CHAPTER 4

How to Talk to Your Spouse About Wanting a Divorce (as a Stay-at-Home Parent)

For many stay-at-home parents, this is the hardest conversation of all. Before the court paperwork, before the housing logistics, before the co-parenting plans—there's this moment.

The one where you have to say, out loud, "I want a divorce." Whether you've tried to talk about it before or kept it buried deep for years, this chapter will walk you through how to prepare for this conversation—emotionally, practically, and safely. Because this moment matters—and you don't have to go into it unarmed.

First, Get Clear With Yourself

Before you say anything to your spouse, get grounded in your decision. You don't need to have every detail mapped out, but you should feel certain enough that this is a conversation worth having.

Ask yourself:

- Am I sure this is what I want—or am I still exploring?
- What outcome am I hoping for in this conversation—clarity? Respect? Separation?
- Am I emotionally safe enough to have this talk in person?
- Do I need a witness, backup plan, or support on standby?

Write it down. Say it out loud to yourself. Feel your body's reaction. This is not a threat—it's a truth. And you deserve to speak it.

If you're unsure what support you might need or how to get started, you can schedule a free 15-minute 1:1 session with our CEO, Olivia. She'll help you connect to the right resources—whether that's legal, emotional, financial, or logistical support. You don't have to figure this out alone.

Signs You Should Not Have This Conversation Alone

If any of the following sound familiar, take extra care. You may want to delay the conversation and create a safety plan before you proceed:

- Your partner has a history of yelling, rage, or controlling behavior
- You've been cut off from your friends or family
- They monitor your phone, computer, or online accounts
- You're afraid they'll cut off your access to money
- You're afraid they'll kick you out or keep the kids from you
- You fear physical retaliation, intimidation, or emotional outbursts
- You've been made to feel unstable or incapable when expressing concerns

If any of these are true, you are not being dramatic. You are being careful. And that's incredibly smart.

Safety Planning Before the Conversation

You do not owe your spouse a heads-up before you're ready. You are allowed to prepare first. In fact, we encourage it—because your safety, stability, and sense of control matter deeply.

Here are some practical steps to consider:

Call a domestic violence hotline even if you're unsure whether your situation "qualifies." These organizations are trained to help people navigate emotionally and financially controlling relationships. They won't judge you—they'll help you make a plan.

Have someone nearby or on standby when you share the news. Whether it's a trusted friend in the next room, a sibling on the phone, or someone waiting for a check-in text, having a support person can make a big difference.

Consider writing a letter or having the conversation in therapy. You don't have to sit down face-to-face if that feels unsafe. A letter, an email, or a therapist-supported setting can help create structure and reduce emotional volatility.

Prepare a "go bag." Include essentials like a change of clothes for you and your kids, copies of important documents, keys, medication, emergency cash or gift cards, and phone numbers written on paper.

Don't share your plans until legal or housing steps are in motion. If you suspect your spouse might retaliate—by locking you out, draining bank accounts, or escalating emotionally—wait until you've filed for temporary orders, secured a place to stay, or connected with legal aid.

Use a secure, private email and cloud storage. Keep all sensitive documents, legal communication, and safety plans in an account that only you can access—ideally on a device your spouse doesn't control.

You Are Not Alone

If you are in immediate danger, or simply need to talk through your situation, help is available 24/7.

National Domestic Violence Hotline

Call 800-799-7233 or text "START" to 88788

Free. Confidential. Judgment-free.

There is nothing wrong with protecting yourself. You are not overreacting. You are taking the first brave step toward building a safer, more stable life.

You deserve support. You deserve safety. And you are not alone.

Choosing the Right Time and Place

This conversation deserves more than a drive-by on the way to soccer practice. Choose your timing intentionally.

Tips:

- Don't do it in the heat of an argument

- Avoid holidays, birthdays, or emotionally loaded days

- Choose a time when the kids aren't home or can't overhear

- If needed, suggest a neutral location (a parked car, therapist's office, etc.)

- Have a backup plan if things go badly (can you leave the room? do you have a friend who knows you're having the conversation?)

This isn't about controlling the reaction—it's about setting you up for stability.

Scripts for Starting the Conversation

Let's be real: nothing makes this easy. But you don't have to go in cold. These scripts are adaptable—choose what fits your voice and relationship.

"I need to talk to you about something I've been holding in for a long time. I've made the decision that I want to end our marriage. I've thought a lot about this, and it's not something I'm saying out of anger—it's something I believe is the right path forward for me."

"This is one of the hardest things I've ever had to say. I want a divorce. I know this might come as a shock, but this is something I've been quietly working through for a long time. I'm not blaming you. I'm just ready for change."

"I know this isn't the conversation either of us wants to have, but I've made the decision to separate. I've already made arrangements to stay somewhere safe and focus on next steps. I'm open to respectful communication going forward."

"I've spent a lot of time reflecting, and I need to talk to you about something important. I've come to the decision that I need to end our marriage. This isn't about blame—it's about growth and honesty. I hope we can navigate this with respect and care for each other."

"I'm not happy in this marriage, and I don't see a way forward together. I want a divorce. I've thought this through carefully, and I'm taking steps to move forward in a safe and stable way for me and the kids."

"This is incredibly difficult for me to say, but I need to be honest with you. I want to separate and begin the process of divorce. I know this will be hard, but I believe we both deserve a future where we feel fulfilled and supported."

"I'm scared to say this out loud, but I've been carrying this for a while. I want to get divorced. I've tried so hard to make things work, but I can't keep pretending I'm okay. I'm not. I'm choosing a different path for myself and for our family's future."

"I've made the decision to leave the marriage, and I've already taken steps to prepare. I've secured a safe place to stay and support to help me through this process. I'd like to keep things as calm and respectful as possible for the sake of everyone involved."

"I still care about you, and I always will. But I've realized that this marriage isn't the right place for me anymore. I'm asking for a divorce—not to hurt you, but to be honest with myself and give us both a chance to rebuild."

"I need to let you know that I'm ending the marriage. This is not up for debate. I have a plan in place to make this transition as peaceful and safe as possible. I will communicate through appropriate channels moving forward."

"I know this is going to change everything, but I want you to know I've thought long and hard about what's best for me and the kids. I've decided to pursue a divorce. I believe we can still be good co-parents, even if we're not partners."

"I've given this a lot of thought, and I've come to the decision that I want to separate and move forward with a divorce. This isn't just about us—it's about creating a healthier environment for the kids, too. I'm committed to co-parenting in a respectful, stable way so they feel safe and supported."

"This is going to be a big change for all of us, and I want to be honest with you. I want a divorce. It's not something I take lightly, especially because of the kids. But I believe we can find a way to make this work so they continue to feel loved and secure."

"I've made the decision to end our marriage, and I want to talk about how we can do this in a way that keeps the kids at the center. They need consistency and peace, and I believe we can work together to give them that—even if we're not together as a couple anymore."

"This isn't easy to say, but I believe it's time for us to move in separate directions. I want a divorce. Our relationship isn't what it used to be, and I want to model something better—for both ourselves and the kids. They deserve two parents who are emotionally healthy, even if that means living in two different homes."

"I've spent a long time thinking about what's best—not just for me, but for the kids too. I've made the decision to move forward with a divorce. I'm not looking for conflict. I want to focus on how we can both be steady, supportive parents through this change."

"I want to talk to you about something difficult. I've reached the decision to divorce, and I'd like us to find a path forward that prioritizes the kids' stability and peace. I hope we can work together on next steps in a way that supports all of us."

What to Expect (and How to Stay Grounded)

Here's what might happen:

- They might cry.

- They might rage.

- They might gaslight you.

- They might beg.

- They might say nothing.
- They might say "Me too."

Whatever the reaction: you are allowed to stay calm and clear.

Remind yourself:

- "Their reaction is not my responsibility."
- "I can stay in control of my tone, my timing, and my energy."
- "I don't have to make decisions beyond this conversation today."
- "This is the first step—not the full sprint."

If they're angry or yelling:

"I understand this is upsetting. I didn't expect this to be easy for either of us. I'm not going to argue or raise my voice. I'm open to talking more when things feel calmer."

"I can hear that you're upset. I'm not trying to hurt you. I've made this decision thoughtfully, and I'm going to continue to speak from a place of respect and care—for both of us and the kids."

If they lash out or try to guilt you:

"I know this hurts, and I'm sorry that it does. But I'm allowed to make a decision that's right for me, even if it's hard for you to understand right now."

"I'm not going to defend my decision over and over. I didn't come to this lightly, and this isn't a punishment—it's a change that I need to make for my well-being."

If they say things like "you're ruining the family" or "you're selfish":

"I know it feels that way to you right now. But choosing to leave a marriage that no longer works is not selfish—it's honest. I believe the kids will benefit from two parents who are living more peacefully, even if it's separately."

"This isn't about ruining the family. It's about rebuilding something healthier—for all of us. I still believe we can be good parents, even if we're no longer partners."

If they threaten you or try to scare you (e.g., about custody or finances):

"I'm taking steps to make sure this process is handled fairly and legally. If we need to talk about parenting or finances, we can do it through the appropriate channels."

"This is exactly why I've lined up support. I want to move forward peacefully, but I'm not going to be intimidated or manipulated."

If they're emotionally devastated or begging:

"I didn't want to hurt you, and I know this is incredibly painful. But I've made my decision. I hope in time you'll understand that this isn't about you—it's about me choosing a new path."

"I hear how much you're hurting. I'm not trying to erase our history. But I can't stay in this marriage just because it's hard to leave. I need to do what's right for me and for the future."

If they try to argue or debate the decision:

"This isn't a debate. I've made my decision, and I'm not going to keep revisiting it. I'm willing to talk about logistics and next steps, but I won't argue about whether or not this is happening."

"We may not agree, but I'm clear on what I need to do. We can work together on the next steps, but my decision stands."

What Comes After the Conversation?

You've said the words. You've opened the door. Now what?

First, breathe.

Even if your partner reacted calmly, you may feel emotionally flooded, shaky, or exhausted.

That's normal. This is a massive moment, and your body and brain need time to process.

You do not need to jump into logistics right away.

You do not owe anyone a second conversation before you're ready.

You are allowed to pause.

Immediate Next Steps (within the first few days):

Regulate your nervous system. Go for a walk, take deep breaths, call a trusted friend, or write it all out.

Prioritize physical and emotional safety. If you don't feel safe, take steps to protect yourself and your children. That may include staying elsewhere, contacting a DV hotline, or speaking with a professional.

Document the conversation. Write down what you said, what was said in return, and any concerning behavior.

Reach out for support. This could mean scheduling a free 15-minute 1:1 with Olivia, connecting with a therapist, or calling a legal aid organization.

What if your partner keeps trying to talk about it?

It's common for partners—especially those who didn't see it coming—to want to talk about it again and again. But repetition doesn't lead to resolution. It just drains you.

Here's what you can say if you're not ready for more discussion yet:

If you need space:

"I know this is a lot to process. It is for me too. I need some space right now before we talk more."

"I'm not ready to keep discussing this. We both need some time to think and calm down before we revisit it."

If they keep trying to revisit the decision:

"I'm not going to keep going in circles. I've made my decision, and it's okay if you need time to come to terms with it."

"I hear that you're upset, but I'm not available for more conversations about this today."

"We can talk about next steps when we're both calmer. Right now, I'm focusing on stabilizing things for myself and the kids."

If you feel unsafe or like they're trying to manipulate you:

"I'm not going to be pressured into continuing a conversation that's harming my mental health. I'll speak with you through a neutral third party going forward."

"This isn't a productive or respectful space right now. I'll be stepping away from the conversation."

Gentle Reminder for You

You don't need to go back to "normal life" right away. You don't need to cook dinner and pretend nothing happened. It's okay to take space, change the routine, and hold your boundaries firmly. Your safety, clarity, and emotional stability matter—now more than ever.

What NOT to Reveal Yet

You may feel pressure to answer every question—but you don't have to.

Here's what you are not obligated to share right away:

- Where you'll live
- Whether you'll file first
- Whether you've talked to a lawyer
- Financial details or plans
- Custody ideas

If they press, try:

- "I'm still figuring that out."

- "I'll share more when I'm ready."

- "That's something we'll work through when the time comes."

Aftercare for Yourself

This conversation takes a lot out of you. Don't pretend it didn't. Whether it went well, badly, or somewhere in between—you just took a massive step toward your future.

After the conversation:

- Text a friend or therapist: "It's done."

- Do something that grounds you—walk, cry, shower, journal.

- Remind yourself you are not alone.

- Open this book back up, and we'll keep going.

- You don't have to be perfect. You don't have to be fearless.

- You just have to be honest. And you just were. That's enough.

We're proud of you. Let's keep going.

CHAPTER 5

———

Asking for Help (Financial + Logistical)

Let's be honest—this might be the chapter that makes you the most uncomfortable. If you've been a stay-at-home parent, you've likely been the one giving help, not asking for it. You may feel like you "should" be able to figure it out alone. But here's the truth: divorce is not a solo mission. Whether you need a few hundred dollars, a safe place to stay, childcare, or just someone to witness your experience—asking for help is not a weakness. It's a strategy.

In this chapter, we'll walk you through who to ask, how to ask, and what kinds of support are realistic to request. You don't have to ask for everything. But you can ask for something.

Who Can You Ask?

Start by identifying people in your world who:

- Know you and your kids
- Have helped you in small ways before
- Are emotionally safe (don't shame, blame, or gossip)
- Have access to time, skills, or resources you don't

These might include:

- A sibling, cousin, or close friend
- Your child's teacher, principal, or daycare provider
- A neighbor, parent at school, or church member
- A therapist, social worker, or school counselor
- A community support group or nonprofit org

Need Help Now? Nonprofit Support Organizations & Shelters Can Be a Lifeline

What Are Nonprofit Support Organizations & Shelters?

They are community-based resources designed to support people (especially women and children) during crisis moments like domestic violence, financial hardship, housing instability, or divorce.

They may offer:

- Free or sliding-scale legal aid
- Emergency shelter or transitional housing
- Transportation to court or appointments
- Food, diapers, clothing, hygiene supplies
- Support groups and counseling
- Connections to pro bono attorneys and social workers

Why This Is a Smart Move

- You get immediate, real-world help with the things you need most

- They often have deep networks of legal, medical, and housing professionals

- You'll work with people who understand trauma, control, and life transitions

- These services are often confidential and free of charge

Whether you're seeking safety, clarity, or a fresh start—these resources can make a life-changing difference.

Simple Scripts for How to Ask for Help

Step 1: Call 211 or Visit 211.org

211 is a free, nationwide hotline that connects you to local social services, including shelters, legal aid, and emergency support.

Phone Script: "Hi, I'm looking for help with [a divorce / leaving a controlling relationship / legal support / housing] and I'm not sure where to start. Can you help connect me to any local nonprofits or shelters that offer support?"

Step 2: Call The Hotline (24/7 Confidential Support)

If you are in an unsafe or emotionally abusive situation, call The National Domestic Violence Hotline at 800-799-SAFE (7233).

Phone Script: "Hi, I need help figuring out my next steps. I'm in a situation that feels unsafe, and I'm considering leaving. I don't know where to go or what to do, but I'd like to talk to someone."

You don't need proof of abuse. You don't need a plan. You just need to call.

Step 3: Contact Local Nonprofits

Look for:

- YWCA chapters

- Women's crisis centers

- Parenting and family support centers

- Local legal aid societies

You can say: "Hi, I'm reaching out because I'm going through a really hard time and need support. Do you offer help with [legal resources / housing / transportation / safety planning] or can you refer me to someone who does?"

What to Expect (and What to Have Ready)

These organizations are trauma-informed and will walk you through the process gently. They may ask for:

- ○ Your first name only (confidentiality is a priority)

- ○ A brief description of your current situation

- ○ Any immediate needs (shelter, court dates, etc.)

You do not need to have everything figured out. You just need to take that first step.

Many women feel stuck because they don't know help exists—or they're afraid to ask. Nonprofits and shelters aren't just for worst-case scenarios. They're for anyone who needs a safe, supported space to land.

They can help you get:

- A ride to court

- A lawyer to review your paperwork

- A place to sleep for the night

- A plan for what happens next

This is your reminder: You are not a burden. You are not alone. You are allowed to ask for help.

Quick Links to Get Started

Call 211 or visit 211.org for local support

The Hotline: 800-799-SAFE or thehotline.org

Find a local YWCA: ywca.org

Legal Aid Directory: https://www.napaba.org/page/nat_leg_aid_dir/NATIONAL-LEGAL-AID-DIRECTORY.htm

Find pro bono help: probono.net

It's not just about surviving—it's about rebuilding with dignity, hope, and the right support.

Whether you need a place to stay, a lawyer to call, or someone to simply say, "I believe you," nonprofit support organizations and shelters are here for you.

There is help. There is a path forward. And you don't have to take the first step alone.

What Kind of Help Can You Ask For?

You're not asking someone to fund your whole divorce or solve everything. You're asking for a small piece of help—just enough to get you to the next step.

Here are real, common asks:

- "Can you watch the kids while I go to court / legal aid / job interview?"

- "Can you loan me $100 to pay for a filing fee or groceries this week?"

- "Can I sleep on your couch for two nights if things get rough?"

- "Can I use your mailing address for some sensitive paperwork?"

- "Can you write a short letter saying I've been the kids' primary caregiver?"

These are reasonable. These are survivable. And you deserve this support.

How to Borrow Money from Friends or Family to Start the Divorce Process (Without Burning Bridges)

When you're ready to move forward with a divorce but don't have the funds to cover filing fees or legal help, it can feel like you're stuck. One option many people overlook is turning to a trusted friend or family member for a short-term loan—with a clear, respectful repayment plan in place.

It might feel uncomfortable at first, but with honesty, structure, and follow-through, borrowing from someone you trust can be a smart, empowering solution.

Asking a loved one for temporary financial help so you can cover the immediate costs of starting your divorce—like filing fees, service fees, or initial legal consultations.

This isn't asking for a handout. It's asking for a bridge—a way to move forward now while planning to pay them back soon.

Why This Is a Smart Option

- It gives you immediate access to legal support

- You avoid high-interest credit cards or predatory loans

- It lets you take action without waiting for "perfect" circumstances

- You can create a clear repayment plan that respects both parties

Scripts and Tips for How to Ask for Financial Help from People in Your Life

Whether you ask over the phone or in person, the key is to be honest, specific, and prepared. Here's how to approach the conversation:

Conversation Script: Asking for Help Respectfully

"I want to talk to you about something that's hard for me to ask. I'm trying to move forward with filing for divorce, and I don't have the money to cover the court costs right now. I need about $500 to file and serve the papers. I'm asking if you'd be open to lending it to me short-term—I can repay $100 per month starting in [month]."

Optional Add-On: "I'm happy to write up a repayment agreement or track everything in writing so we both feel comfortable."

Tips for a Smooth Conversation

- Be transparent about how the money will be used

- Offer a specific repayment plan and timeline

- Respect a "no"—not everyone is in a place to help, and that's okay

- Follow up in writing to confirm the details if they say yes

Make It Official (Even If It's Informal)

To avoid tension later, put the agreement in writing. It doesn't have to be complicated.

Here's a basic sample:

Simple Loan Agreement Example

Date: [MM/DD/YYYY] | Borrower: [Your Name]

Lender: [Their Name] | Loan Amount: $500

Repayment Plan: $100/month, starting [Month, Year]

Final Payment Due: [Final Month, Year]

Notes: Payments will be made via [Venmo / PayPal / Cash / Bank Transfer].

Signatures:

_____ (Your Name)   _____ (Their Name)

Action Steps to Get Started

Make a list of trusted people you feel safe asking (think emotionally supportive + financially stable)

- Write out exactly what you need and when you can repay

- Practice your ask—whether it's a phone call, text, or in-person conversation

- Be clear about the purpose of the funds (filing fees, legal advice, etc.)

- Put it in writing once agreed to protect both sides

Real Talk: It's Okay to Ask for Help

Asking for money can feel vulnerable—but this is about investing in your future, your safety, and your peace of mind. People who love you want to see you move forward. When you come prepared and respectful, it shows you're taking your next chapter seriously.

Legal support shouldn't be out of reach just because you're in a hard financial season.

Borrowing from someone who believes in you—with a clear plan to pay them back—can give you the breathing room to move forward with confidence.

And remember: you're not failing by asking for support—you're taking a bold, empowered step toward your fresh start.

Script Bank: What to Say When Asking for Help

Asking for Financial Support

"I'm going through a divorce and I'm trying to take the next steps. I'm in a tough financial spot right now. Would you be open to loaning me $100 to help with [filing fees / groceries / transportation]? I would never ask if I didn't really need it."

"Hey, this feels so awkward to ask, but I'm in the thick of divorce stuff and kind of drowning financially. Would you be able to lend me $100 to help with [filing fees / groceries / transportation]? I wouldn't ask unless I really had to. Totally okay if it's not doable—I just figured I'd ask."

"Hey [Name], I'm going through a divorce right now and trying to manage some unexpected expenses. I'm in a tough financial spot and looking for $100 to cover [filing fees / groceries / transportation]. If you're in a position to help, I'd be deeply grateful—and if not, totally understood. If you happen to know someone who might be open to helping or offering a short-term loan, feel free to pass this along."

"Hi [Name], I'm going through a divorce right now and it's been really hard financially. I'm wondering if you'd be open to loaning me $100 to help with [filing fees / groceries / transportation]? I could pay you back by [specific date or "next month"]. I wouldn't ask if it wasn't important—thank you for even considering it."

"Hey [Name], I'm learning to ask for support when I need it—and right now, I do. I'm going through a divorce and trying to stay steady, but financially it's really hard. If you'd be open to loaning me $100 to help with [filing fees / groceries / transportation], I would be so grateful. No pressure at all—just trying to meet this moment with honesty and care."

Asking for a Safe Place to Stay

"I may need a backup place to stay for a few nights if things get difficult at home. I don't want to put you in an uncomfortable position, but I'm trying to make a safety plan and I wanted to ask if I could count on you as an option."

"Hey [Name], I'm working on a safety plan as I navigate some stuff at home, and I wanted to ask something that's not easy to bring up. If things get hard, would it be okay if I considered your place as a backup to stay for a night or two? I completely understand if it's not doable—I just wanted to ask rather than assume."

"Hi [Name], I'm trying to put a plan in place in case things escalate at home. Would you be open to me staying at your place for a couple nights if needed? I totally understand if it's not possible—I just want to make sure I have a few safe options lined up."

"Hey, I feel a little nervous asking this, but I'm working on a safety plan and want to be prepared if things at home become too difficult. Would you be okay with me reaching out to stay with you for a night or two if it comes to that? No pressure—I just need to know where I can land if I need to."

"Hey [Name], I'm working on a safety plan just in case things at home get difficult. I wanted to ask if you'd be open to me and the kids staying with you for a night or two if we needed a backup place. I truly don't want to put you out, and I hope we won't need it—but knowing we have that option would mean a lot."

"I've been trying to create a plan to make sure me and the kids have somewhere safe to go if things get tough at home. I hate to even ask, but would it be okay to consider your place as a short-term backup? Just a night or two if needed. I'd never ask unless I really needed it."

"Hey [Name], I'm hoping we won't need it, but I'm trying to line up a safe option for me and the kids to stay somewhere temporarily if home gets hard. Could I check in with you as a backup, just for a night or two? I know it's a big ask, and I'd totally understand if it's not a good time."

Asking for Childcare Help

"Would you be open to helping me with a few hours of childcare? I have to attend a legal appointment and I don't have coverage. I'd be happy to trade or repay in another way—this would really help me."

"Hey! Any chance you'd be able to help me with a couple hours of childcare? I've got a legal thing I need to be at and I'm stuck without coverage. Happy to repay the favor however I can— really appreciate you even considering it!"

"I've got a legal appointment and no childcare that day, and I'm trying to line up someone I trust. Would you be open to helping for a couple hours? I'd be so grateful and absolutely want to trade or support you in return."

"Hey! I'm in a bit of a pinch and was wondering if you'd be able to help watch the kids for a few hours while I go to a legal appointment. Totally happy to swap for a favor, errand, or future babysitting. Let me know if that might be possible!"

"Hi [Name], I hope it's okay to reach out with a quick ask. I have a legal appointment coming up and I'm trying to find short-term childcare coverage. Would you happen to be available for a few hours that day? No worries at all if not—I completely understand. I'd be happy to trade time or help in return."

"Hey [Mom/Dad/etc.], I have a legal appointment coming up and I could really use help with the kids for a few hours. I'll make sure everything's set up and easy for you—it would be such a relief to know they're with someone they know. Let me know if that's something you'd be open to."

"Hey [Name], I have a legal appointment on [date/time] and I'm in need of childcare for [number] hours. The kids would be at home and already fed, and I'll leave everything prepped. Would you be open to helping? I can offer trade, payment, or any support in return. No pressure—just reaching out to see if it's something that might work for you."

How to Request a Letter Confirming Your Role as Primary Parent (and Why It Matters)

When you're navigating a divorce or custody situation—especially if you've been a stay-at-home parent or haven't had traditional employment—proving your role as the primary caregiver can be incredibly important. While legal documents and financials often dominate the process, letters from people who have seen you parent firsthand can offer powerful, real-life evidence of your role in your child's day-to-day life.

Why These Letters Matter

If you've spent most of your time raising your children—managing their schedules, attending school meetings, staying home when they're sick—you've been doing full-time caregiving work, even if it hasn't shown up on a paycheck. Unfortunately, the legal system doesn't always account for this unpaid labor unless it's documented. That's where these letters come in.

A simple statement from a teacher, neighbor, family member, or family friend can go a long way in demonstrating your caregiving role. These letters can:

- Support custody arrangements by showing you've been the primary, consistent caregiver.

- Offset lack of financial records if you haven't been employed or if you worked part-time.

- Add weight to your divorce filing, especially if you're representing yourself or working with legal aid.

Who to Ask

The best letters come from people who have directly observed you parenting. That might include:

- Teachers or school administrators

- Pediatricians or therapists (if they're willing)

- Family friends who've spent time in your home

- Babysitters or nannies who've worked alongside you

- Neighbors or relatives who've witnessed your daily routines

- These don't need to be formal professionals—honest, firsthand accounts are just as powerful.

How to Ask for a Letter of Support

You don't need to overthink it. A simple, respectful ask works best. Here's some sample messages you can use (text, email, or in person):

"Would you feel comfortable writing a short letter stating that you've witnessed me being the primary caregiver for my kids? It doesn't need to be fancy—just a few sentences about what you've seen, like me handling school drop-offs, meals, appointments, or routines. I'm putting together some documentation for my custody process, and your perspective would really help."

"Hey! Quick question—would you be up for writing a short note saying you've seen me doing the day-to-day parenting stuff? Just something simple about what you've noticed. I'm putting together paperwork for custody and it would mean a lot."

"I'm working on some custody documentation right now, and part of that includes showing I've been the primary caregiver. Would you be open to writing a short letter about what you've observed—things like school stuff, medical appointments, daily routines, etc.? Just a few sentences would really help."

"Hi [Name], I'm currently in the process of preparing some legal paperwork related to custody, and I'm collecting a few short letters from people who've seen me in my role as primary caregiver. If you're comfortable, would you be willing to write a brief note confirming what you've observed in terms of my involvement in day-to-day parenting or school coordination? I completely understand if that's not something you're able to do—just thought I'd ask."

"This feels a little awkward to ask, but would you be comfortable writing a short letter saying you've witnessed me as the main caregiver for the kids? I'm putting together some documents for court, and your words would really help me show the reality of what our day-to-day looks like."

"Hi [Name], I completely understand that your role is bound by confidentiality, but I'm checking in to see if you're permitted—and feel comfortable—providing a brief letter confirming my consistent presence and involvement as the primary caregiver during appointments. I'm preparing custody documentation and gathering support letters from those who've seen me in a caregiving role. I understand fully if this is outside what you're able to do."

Most people want to help—you just need to make it easy for them.

What the Letter Should Include

Keep it short and factual. Here's a sample you can share:

Sample Letter Template:

"I have known [Your Name] for [X] years and have regularly observed them as the primary caregiver to their children. They have been responsible for day-to-day care, school coordination, medical appointments, and household routines. It is clear to me that they have served as the children's main parent and source of support."

The letter should be signed and dated if possible. A PDF, an email, or even a handwritten note is acceptable—just make sure you save a copy.

Final Tips

- Keep a list of who you've asked and when they responded.

- Thank people for their time and support—this is an emotional process for everyone.

- Save copies of every letter you receive, and share them with your lawyer or legal aid team.

You don't have to prove your parenting with fancy spreadsheets or job titles. You've been there. These letters help tell that story.

CHAPTER 6

———

Talking to People About Your Divorce

Divorce doesn't happen in a vacuum. It touches everything—school pick-up lines, text threads with friends, your spot at the PTA table. And if you're a stay-at-home parent, that ripple can feel more like a tidal wave. You might be wondering: Will people whisper? Will they side-eye? Will they ask too many questions—or none at all?

This chapter is here to help you navigate those conversations with clarity and care. Whether you're talking to your kids, giving your friend the quick version over text, or letting the school know what's changed, we've got scripts, tools, and boundaries to help you share what you want to share—on your terms.

Who You Have to Tell (and Who You Don't)

Let's start here: you don't owe your story to everyone.

You do not have to explain yourself to your in-laws, your bossy neighbor, or the PTA. But there are people you may need to tell for legal, logistical, or emotional reasons.

Here's who to prioritize:

- Your children (in age-appropriate ways)

- Your child's school or daycare

- Healthcare providers (especially pediatricians and therapists)

- Friends or family members who are part of your support system

Everyone else? Optional.

Not sure what to say? We've got you covered with scripts for each convo. Let's get started.

Talking to Your Kids About the Divorce

Here's the truth: 90% of talking to kids about divorce is your energy. If you can come to the conversation with calm, clarity, and a sense of grounded love, your child will feel that—maybe even more than the words you say. That's why we highly recommend reading through this next part before starting the conversation. Your child might be confused, curious, or totally unfazed in the moment. They might cry, get angry, or go quiet. However they respond, it's okay. Your job isn't to fix their feelings—it's to stay present, loving, and steady. Remember, divorce is a process, not a one-time event. You have plenty of time to grow through this together.

When it comes to telling your kids about the divorce, setting the stage thoughtfully can make a big difference. Choose a quiet, calm time—ideally when no one is rushing out the door or winding down for sleep. A familiar space like the living room or kitchen table can help kids feel more secure. Sit together at their level, if you can—on the couch, the floor, or wherever feels natural and connected. You want to communicate, not just with your words, but with your presence: We are here. You are safe. You are loved.

If it's possible, both parents should be present. It sends the message that, even though the relationship between the grown-ups is changing, you are still united in your love and care for your child. Keep the messaging simple and consistent. Rehearse what you're going to say if you need to. And if one parent isn't willing or able to be there for the conversation, that's okay too. You can still offer your child a safe, loving explanation in a calm tone. What matters most is that you are regulated and emotionally available.

There is no "perfect" way to have this conversation—there is only the path that honors your family's truth while holding your child with care. They don't need the details right now. They need your steadiness, your love, and your reassurance that even though things are changing, they are not being left behind. You've got this. And we're here to help every step of the way.

Let's begin by breaking down how to talk to the divorce to your kids – by age:

Telling Kids Ages 2–4 About Divorce

For toddlers and preschoolers (around ages 2–4), the key is to keep things simple, soft, and full of love. Olivia's younger son was not even three when she had this conversation—and it took years before he really understood what divorce meant. At this age, kids don't need the big-picture explanation. What they need is reassurance about what's right in front of them: Who's putting me to bed? Where will my toys be? Are we still having pancakes on Saturday? Focus on the immediate changes you know are happening and speak to what they can actually see, feel, and experience. Keep your words rooted in safety, love, and routine—and let the rest unfold in time.

Scripts:

"Hey buddy, we need to tell you something new. Mama and Dada are going to have their own separate houses. That might sound weird, huh? But we both love you so, so much, and that will never ever change. You'll still see both of us, and you'll be taken care of every single day—just like always."

"My love, did you know there are lots of different kinds of families? Some families have one home, and some have two. Mommy and Mama will live in two houses now—but you'll have your own cozy space in both. You are safe in both homes. And no matter where you are, you are so, so loved."

"Hey lovebug. Our family is going through a little change. Daddy and Papa will each have their own house now. That means sometimes you'll live with Daddy, and sometimes with Papa—just like having two superhero bases! And guess what? No matter which house you're in, you are safe, so loved, and always our lovebug."

"Sweetie, we need to tell you something important. Our family is going through a little change, and Mommy and Daddy are going to have their own separate houses. That might sound a little weird or confusing, huh? But guess what—there are all kinds of families. Some have one home, and some have two. You're going to have two cozy homes now—one with Mommy and one with Daddy—just like having two superhero bases! You'll have your special things in both places, and your days will still have hugs, stories, and pancakes. And the most important thing? No matter where you are, you are safe, so, so loved, and always our cuddly, loveable little mouse."

Questions They Might Ask (or Show Through Behavior)

"Where will I live?"

Answer: "You'll have two homes now! One with Mama and one with Dada. You'll have your toys and clothes in both places, and we'll make sure you always know where you're going. And you can still have Sunday pancakes at each house!"

"That's a really good question, sweetheart. You'll have a cozy space in both homes—one with Mommy and one with Mama. Your toys, your snuggly blanket, and your bedtime stories will be there too. You'll go back and forth, and we'll always make sure you know what's happening. Wherever you are, you'll be safe, cared for, and so, so loved."

"That's an excellent question, lovebug. You're going to live in both houses—Daddy's house and Papa's house. You'll have your bed, your toys, and your hugs in each place. And to help you know where you'll be each day, we made a special calendar just for you! It has pictures and colors so you can see who you'll be with and when. We'll look at it together every day so there are no surprises. No matter where you sleep at night, Daddy and Papa will always make sure you feel safe, cozy, and so loved."

If you don't know or if one parent may be moving far: "That's a really good question, sweetheart. Right now, we're still figuring out the details, but what we do know is that you are going to be safe, loved, and taken care of no matter what. Mommy and Daddy both love you so much, and we are going to make sure you always know what's happening and where you'll be. You don't have to worry about grown-up things—we will make sure your days have hugs, your favorite things, and people who love you. If you ever feel confused, you can always ask us. We're here to help you understand everything, one step at a time."

Tip: You can use a visual calendar or routine chart to show them which days they'll be where, or if a parent lives far away, when the FaceTime routine will be.

"Why?"

Answer: "Why is a great question, and this decision is a grown-up choice. We're not happy living in the same house, and it's better for us to live in different homes. But we both love you so much, and that part will never change."

"Are you mad at me?"

Answer: "No, sweetheart. This is not about you. Mommy and Daddy are working on grown-up things, and we both love you more than anything in the world."

"Will I see you every day?"

Answer: "You'll see both of us often. Even when we're not in the same house, we'll always make sure you're safe, loved, and taken care of."

Key Phrases to Repeat Often

- "This is not your fault."

- "You are safe."

- "You are so loved by both of us."

- "We will always take care of you."

- "We're still a family, even if our family looks different now."

Extra Support Ideas

- Let them help decorate or set up their space in each home.

- Offer a transition object (like a stuffie or blanket that goes back and forth).

- Read children's books to normalize divorce (see list in back of book)

- Stick to consistent routines and bedtime rituals to build stability.

Telling Kids Ages 5–8 About Divorce

For children ages 5–8, you'll want to offer a little more detail than with toddlers, but still keep your language simple, clear, and emotionally grounded. Kids this age may ask more direct questions, worry about blame or loyalty, and need extra reassurance around routine, love, and safety.

Scripts:

"We want to talk to you about something important. Mommy and Mama have decided that we're going to live in different houses. We're not going to be married anymore, but we will always be your parents, and we will always love you. Our love for you never changes."

"We have something important to tell you. Dad and I have decided we won't be married anymore, and we'll be living in two different homes. But no matter what, we are still your parents—and we both love you more than anything. That will never, ever change."

Questions They Might Ask (or Think But Not Say)

"Why are you getting divorced?"

Answer: "Sometimes grown-ups stop getting along in the way married people need to. We've tried to fix it, but we decided it's better for everyone if we live separately. This is not something you caused, and it's not something you can fix. It's our job to take care of you."

"Can you get back together?"

Answer: "No, we're not going to be married again, even though we'll both always be your parents, and that will never change. We've made this decision because we believe it's best for our whole family, even if it feels hard right now."

Find the Experts you need at freshstartsregistry.com/experts

"Is it my fault?"

Answer: "No, not even a little bit. This is a grown-up decision, and you didn't do anything wrong. We love you no matter what."

"What's going to happen to me?"

Answer: "What a brave question to ask! You're still going to go to school, play with your friends, and do all the things you love. We'll make sure you always know where you're going to be, and you'll be taken care of every day."

Key Phrases to Repeat Often

- "You didn't cause this."

- "We love you so much."

- "You can ask us any questions, anytime."

- "We're always going to be your parents."

- "You're safe, and we're here for you."

Extra Support Ideas

- Encourage them to draw or write about their feelings (even with stick figures).

- Let them help decorate or pack a small "go-bag" of comfort items for each home.

- Reinforce consistency in routines: meals, bedtime, school, and activities.

- Check out the book list in the back of this book for family books on normalizing divorce

Telling Kids Ages 9–12 About Divorce

Kids ages 9–12 are often more emotionally aware, may have big feelings and big questions, and might try to make sense of the divorce logically or morally. They may also worry about loyalty, fairness, and the future, so clarity, emotional validation, and structure are key.

Scripts:

"We want to talk to you about something important. After a lot of thought, we've decided to get a divorce. That means we won't be married anymore, and we'll be living in different homes. But what's not changing is that we're both still your parents—and we both love you so much. That part stays the same, always. This wasn't a quick or easy decision. We've spent a long time trying to figure things out, and we've realized that living apart is what's healthiest for all of us. It's completely normal to have a lot of different feelings about this—confused, sad, mad, even relieved. However you feel is okay, and we're here to talk, listen, and support you through it all."

"We need to share something important with you. After a lot of thinking and talking, we've decided that we're going to separate and not be married anymore. That means we'll be living in different homes, and some things will change—but one thing that never changes is how much we both love you. We're still your parents, and we always will be. This wasn't a decision we made quickly. We really tried to work through things, but we realized that living apart is what's best for our family right now. We know this might bring up a lot of different feelings—maybe sadness, anger, confusion, or even some relief. Whatever you feel is completely okay. We're here to answer your questions, listen to anything you want to share, and walk through this with you, every step of the way."

Questions They Might Ask (or Think But Not Say)

"Why is this happening?"

Answer: "That's a great question. Well, we've had a hard time getting along, and even though we tried to fix things, we realized that separating is the best way forward. It's about how we treat each other as partners—this is not about anything you or your sister did, sometimes grown ups just grow apart, and that's okay."

"Could you just stay together for me?"

Answer: "We know how much you want things to stay the same. We really thought about that too. But staying together when things aren't working doesn't help anyone in the long run. We believe you deserve to grow up in a peaceful home, even if that means two homes."

"Who am I going to live with? What if I don't like the plan?"

Answer: "We're working on a plan that gives you time with both of us. You'll be safe, loved, and cared for no matter what. You can tell us how you feel about the plan—we want to hear from you—but there are also some things that we, as the parents, have to decide."

"Am I supposed to pick sides?"

Answer: "No, and we would never ask you to. This is between the two of us. We both love you so much, and that love is not a competition. You're allowed to love both of us fully, always."

"What's going to change?"

Answer: "Some things will be different, like having two homes or a new routine. But lots of things will stay the same—your school, your friends, your hobbies. We'll work together to keep your life as steady and supported as possible."

Key Phrases to Repeat Often

- "This is not your fault."
- "We're still a family—we just look different now."
- "You don't have to take care of us—we're here to take care of you."
- "You can love both of us, and you never have to choose sides."
- "It's okay to feel confused, angry, or sad. We'll get through this together."

Find the Experts you need at freshstartsregistry.com/experts

Extra Support Ideas

- Create a shared calendar app or physical planner for transitions between homes.

- Offer age-appropriate books to normalize divorce (see in the back of this book)

- Encourage open conversations, journaling, or therapy if they're open to it.

- Let them have some small choices in the transition (what goes to each house, how they decorate their new room, etc.).

Telling Kids Ages 13–15 About Divorce

For kids ages 13–15, you're speaking to young teens who are developing critical thinking, emotional nuance, and independence. They may try to take sides, shut down, or feel pressure to "be mature." They may also have strong opinions and big emotions—but still need just as much reassurance, structure, and permission to feel.

Scripts:

"We need to have a serious conversation with you. After a lot of thought and effort, we've decided to end our marriage. We'll be living separately, but one thing that will never change is that we are your parents—and we love you more than anything. We know this might come with a lot of different emotions—anger, sadness, maybe even confusion or relief—and whatever you feel is valid. You don't need to have it all figured out. We're here to talk, answer your questions honestly, and make sure you feel supported and secure as we move through this together."

"This isn't easy to say, but we've decided to get a divorce. It doesn't mean we don't care about each other—it just means we've realized we're no longer able to be married in a way that's healthy for our family. What hasn't changed is how much we both love you and how committed we are to being your parents. We know you're old enough to understand the weight of this, and we trust your ability to ask questions, have big feelings, and form your own opinions. You don't need to protect us or pretend you're fine. We're still the ones taking care of you, and we're going to get through this together."

Questions They Might Ask (Or Think But Not Say)

"Who made this decision?"

Answer: "That's a great question. This was a joint decision. We've been talking about it for a while, and we both agreed that it was time to make a change for everyone's well-being."

"So, is someone to blame?"

Answer: "I appreciate your questions! Well, there isn't just one reason. Relationships are complex, and this isn't about one person being 'at fault.' We're choosing to end our marriage in a way that's respectful and healthy for the long run."

"What happens to me? Can I choose where I live?"

Answer: "You're old enough that your voice matters, and we want to hear how you feel. Some of the decisions will be based on legal and logistical factors, but we want to work together so that you feel seen, safe, and supported."

"What's going to change—and what's staying the same?"

Answer: "Some things will shift—like which parent you're with on which days—but lots of things will stay the same: your school, your friends, your activities. We'll walk through it together and make sure you have what you need."

"Why now?"

Answer: "We stayed together as long as we felt we could in a healthy way. But the way things have been isn't working anymore—for us, or for the family. We want to model what it looks like to make hard decisions with honesty and care."

Key Phrases to Repeat Often

- "We're still your parents—no matter what."
- "You don't have to protect us or take sides."
- "Your feelings are valid, even if they're big or confusing."
- "We want to hear how you're feeling, whenever you're ready."
- "This isn't something you need to fix or carry."

Extra Support Ideas

- Encourage open dialogue, therapy, or journaling (without forcing it).
- Respect their need for privacy while still checking in consistently.
- Let them help create routines, manage calendars, or set up their space in each home.

Telling Teens Ages 15–18 About Divorce

Teens ages 15–18 are often highly aware of family dynamics and may already suspect something is wrong. They may express independence, feel angry or betrayed, or swing between deep detachment and emotional overwhelm. The goal at this age is to speak with respect and honesty, while reminding them they're still kids—not mediators, fixers, or therapists.

Scripts:

"We want to be upfront with you, because you're old enough to understand what's happening. We've decided to get a divorce. It's been a difficult decision, and not one we made quickly or lightly. While our relationship as a couple is ending, we're still your parents—and we always will be. That's not changing. We know this might bring up a lot for you—anger, sadness, relief, even questions. Whatever you're feeling is valid. You're not expected to manage our emotions or make sense of it all right now. We're here, we love you, and we'll keep showing up for you."

"You've probably sensed something's been off, and we want to be honest with you. We've made the decision to separate and get a divorce. It's a decision we came to after a lot of time, work, and reflection—and while it's painful, we believe it's the best path forward for all of us. This doesn't mean your whole world is falling apart. We're still your parents, and we're still here for you in all the ways that matter. You don't need to take sides, fix anything, or be 'the adult' in this. We've got that part. What we want most is for you to feel supported through the changes ahead."

Questions They Might Ask (Or Keep Inside)

"So what really happened?"

Answer: "Great question, we're willing to share what we can in a way that's appropriate, but we're not going to involve you in all the adult details. What matters most is that this is a decision we made thoughtfully, and we're focused on helping everyone move forward with respect and care."

"Do I have to move or switch schools?"

Answer: "We're doing everything we can to minimize disruption to your day-to-day life. If any changes are necessary, we'll talk through them with you, listen to your concerns, and make sure you're supported through the transition."

"Am I supposed to pick sides or manage this?"

Answer: "No. That's not your job. We're the adults here, and we're handling the logistics. You're allowed to love us both and have a relationship with each of us on your own terms. You don't have to carry any of this emotionally."

"Why didn't you just wait until I moved out?"

Answer: "We understand that this timing may feel hard. But waiting would've just prolonged the pain for everyone. We believe it's better to model healthy decisions and honest communication now, even if it's uncomfortable."

Key Phrases to Repeat Often

- "This isn't your responsibility."
- "You don't have to take care of us—we're here to take care of you."
- "We want to be honest and respectful, not put you in the middle."
- "Whatever you're feeling is valid."
- "You still get to be a teenager—we've got the grown-up stuff."

Extra Support Ideas

- Offer opportunities for independent processing: therapy, journaling, or trusted adult conversations.
- Give them autonomy in how they engage with each parent (when appropriate).
- Keep communication transparent but respectful—no badmouthing, no guilt-tripping.

Recommended Reading List:

- The Truth About Divorce by Ruth Bell
- Now What Do I Do? by Lynn Cassella-Kapusinski

Scripts for everyone else in your life:

Babysitter: Hey Emily, Hope all is well! There's something I wanted to give you a little family update. Jamie and I have decided to get a divorce. It's a big change, but we're committed to making this transition smooth for everyone, especially Hailey and Luke. Things might seem a little different around here for a while, but know that you're still very much needed and appreciated. We'll chat more about it next time you come over, and let me know if you have any questions. Thanks for your understanding! I'm so glad the kids have you right now (I'm so glad we all have you!).

Parents of Childrens' Friends: Hi Imogen, this is Midge. I wanted to let you know about a change happening in our family. Joel and I have decided to get a divorce. It's a big adjustment, but we want to assure you that both of us are fully committed to supporting Ethan through this time. We're prioritizing open communication and a smooth transition. If Ethan ever mentions anything or seems a little off, please know we're working together and would love your support in keeping things positive for them. Let's chat soon!

Neighbors: Hey Imogen, Just wanted to give you a heads up about some upcoming family changes. Joel and I are splitting up. It's a big adjustment, but we're both committed to smooth sailing for the kiddos. Just a heads up in case things seem a little different around here. Keep things positive with Ethan and Esther, though, everything will be okay! Let's catch up soon! x Midge

Children's teachers: Hi Mr. Feeny, I wanted to let you know about a change happening in Cory's family. Alan and I have decided to get divorced. This is a big adjustment for all of us, but we want to assure you that both of us are fully committed to supporting Cory during this time. We're prioritizing open communication and a smooth transition for Cory. If you see any changes in Cory's emotions or behavior in class, please don't hesitate to reach out. We appreciate your understanding and support for our family during this transitional time.

Children's pediatrician: Dr. Greene, I wanted to touch base about an upcoming change in our family. Bobby and I have decided to get a divorce. We know this might be a significant adjustment for Travis, but we want to emphasize that both of us are committed to providing unwavering love and support during this time. We're working together to prioritize open communication and a smooth transition. If you notice any changes in Travis' emotional well-being or behavior during appointments, please don't hesitate to let us know. We appreciate your guidance and support in ensuring Travis feels comfortable and supported throughout this process.

Children's therapist: Dr. Keener, we wanted to update you on a recent development in Sally's life. Don and I have decided to move forward with a divorce. While this is a big change for all of us, we wanted to assure you that both of us are fully committed to supporting Sally's emotional well-being during this transition. We're prioritizing open communication and a smooth adjustment for Sally. We value your guidance and expertise, and if you notice any significant changes in Sally's emotions or behaviors in therapy, please don't hesitate to bring them to our attention. We believe open communication between all of us is crucial in supporting Sally through this time.

Find the Experts you need at freshstartsregistry.com/experts

Telling your family about the divorce:

Telling your parents you're getting divorced can feel almost as overwhelming as going through the divorce itself. Our advice? Choose a moment when things are relatively calm—avoid holidays, high-stress times, or big family gatherings. If you can, tell them in person or on a video call, where they can see your face and hear your tone. Start by naming the change clearly and confidently, and remind them that while this wasn't an easy decision, it was a thoughtful one. It's okay if emotions run high—you don't have to manage their feelings, just your delivery. Stay grounded by taking deep breaths, keeping your tone calm, and focusing on what you need them to know right now. You can always share more details later. And remember: you are allowed to protect your peace, even with family.

Here are some helpful scripts to start the conversation:

"I need to tell you something important, and I want you to hear it with love: I'm getting divorced. This has been a really difficult decision, but I've reached a place where staying in the marriage isn't healthy for me—or for the kids. I've been the one home with them every day, and I've thought through what this will mean for all of us. I'm not asking for advice—I just wanted you to know, and I hope I can count on your support."

"Mom, Dad—I've made the decision to end my marriage. It's not something I came to lightly, but it's the right path forward. Being at home with the kids has given me a lot of time to see things clearly. This is going to be a big change, and I could really use you in my corner."

"I want to let you know that I've decided to get divorced. This isn't a crisis—it's a turning point. I've been a stay-at-home parent for a long time, and while it's going to be an adjustment, I'm taking steps to rebuild safely and responsibly. I'm not looking for permission or judgment—I'm just being honest about where I am and where I'm going."

"I don't know exactly how to say this, but I'm getting divorced. It's been a long time coming, and I've been holding a lot in while trying to be strong for the kids. I've given everything I have to the home and family, and I'm exhausted—but I'm also ready. I need to know that you'll be there for me, even if you don't understand everything right away."

"I want to share something with you because I trust you, but I'm asking that you don't jump in with solutions or judgments. I'm ending my marriage. I've been a full-time caregiver for the kids and I'm taking the steps I need to move forward in a healthy way. I'll let you know what I need as I figure it out, but for now, I just wanted to be honest."

"I'm sharing this because it's part of my reality, not because I'm opening the floor to debate: I'm getting divorced. I've done a lot of thinking, especially as the parent who's been home every day. This is the best thing for me and the kids. I'm handling it with care, and I'll keep you updated as needed—but please respect my process."

"I'm going to be very clear: I'm getting divorced. I've made this decision carefully and quietly as a stay-at-home parent who's seen the full picture. I'm not interested in defending the choice—I'm focused on building a safe, stable next chapter. I'll share what I'm comfortable with in time."

"You've always been there for me, and I hope that won't change now. I'm getting divorced. As a stay-at-home mom, I've been the one carrying a lot of the emotional and household labor, and I've reached a point where I can't keep doing it this way. I'd really appreciate your emotional support while I figure out my next steps."

Scripts for When Your Parents React:

If they say: "But what about the kids?"

"That's exactly why I'm doing this. I've thought about them every single step of the way. I want them to grow up in a peaceful, stable home—even if it looks different than what we imagined."

If they say: "You've never had a job—how will you survive?"

"I know this is scary, but I'm building a support system, and I've already started putting together a plan. I've been managing our household for years—I can learn new skills. I'm not doing this recklessly."

If they say: "Marriage is hard—you just have to stick it out."

"I have stuck it out. For longer than you know. But staying in something unhealthy just because it's hard isn't what's best for me or the kids."

If they say: "I don't agree with this decision."

"I understand this is hard to hear. But I'm not asking for agreement—I'm letting you in because I hope I can count on your love and support."

If they guilt-trip you: "You're ruining your family."

"I'm not ruining anything—I'm making a hard choice to try and save what's left of myself and give my kids a better future. That's not destruction. That's survival."

If they ask: "Can't you just wait until the kids are older?"

"That's what I've been doing. But waiting hasn't made things better—it's just made me more exhausted. There's no perfect time to do this. But there is now."

If they say: "We had no idea anything was wrong."

"That's okay. You weren't supposed to. I've been carrying this quietly because it wasn't safe—or possible—to share. But I'm sharing now because I need support, not secrecy."

If they get angry or defensive:

"I'm not in a place to argue. I've made my decision. If you need time to process, I respect that. But please don't take it out on me. I need peace right now."

Grounding Reminder for You

Repeat to yourself after a hard conversation:

- I don't owe anyone a full explanation in order to deserve support.

- Other people's discomfort does not mean I've made the wrong choice.

- I am allowed to choose what's best for me and my kids—even if others don't understand yet.

Setting Boundaries When People Offer "Help" That Hurts

Not all help is helpful. If someone's response to your request is to shame you, lecture you, or gossip about you—you are allowed to walk away.

Practice saying:

"I appreciate your concern, but I'm not looking for advice right now."

"That's not helpful for me in this moment. I'm focused on practical next steps."

"I'm making decisions based on what's best for me and my kids. I'm not looking for approval."

It's important to remember that you get to decide what kind of support is welcome. Just because someone frames their words or actions as "help" doesn't mean you have to accept it—especially if it makes you feel worse, second-guessed, or judged. You're already carrying enough. Emotional safety matters just as much as physical safety, and that includes protecting your energy from unsolicited advice, moralizing, or guilt trips disguised as concern.

People may mean well, but intention doesn't always equal impact. You don't have to justify your choices, over-explain your situation, or take on other people's discomfort. Boundaries are not rude—they're necessary tools of self-respect.

When someone offers "support" that's actually shaming or self-serving, you are fully within your rights to set a firm, calm boundary—or to simply disengage. Protect your peace. Choose your circle with care. The people who truly support you will listen more than they lecture.

You are not too much for needing support, and you are not ungrateful for being selective about the kind of support you accept.

Your fresh start belongs to you. Let that be your compass.

CHAPTER 7

————

Budgeting Basics for Beginners

If you've been a stay-at-home parent, chances are you haven't been the one managing the money—and not because you're not capable, but because that was the setup. Maybe your partner handled the bills, the taxes, the bank accounts. Maybe you've never had to sit down and build a budget, and now you're staring down a spreadsheet and wondering how anyone makes this work.

We want you to hear this clearly: you are not behind.

You're not bad with money.

You just haven't had the opportunity—or the access—to learn this part yet.

That ends now.

In this chapter, we're going back to the basics. No shame. No judgment. No financial jargon that makes you feel small. Just real-world, stay-at-home-parent-friendly steps to help you take the first steps toward financial clarity.

We'll walk you through how to:

Understand where your money is going (even if there's not much of it)

Prioritize what really needs to be paid first

Track spending in a way that works for your actual life

Build a simple budget, even if your income is irregular or nonexistent right now

You don't need to be a financial expert to take control of your money. You just need to know what matters most, what you can do with what you have, and how to take one small action at a time.

You are not powerless here. In fact, every dollar you track, every account you open, every step you take—it's all part of you building your freedom.

Let's get you there.

What Budgeting Really Is (and What It Isn't)

Let's reframe this word. A budget is not a punishment. It's not a spreadsheet of failure. It's a tool to help you feel safe and in control during a time when everything else might feel chaotic.

A Budget Tells You:

- What your real-life numbers are

- What's urgent and what can wait

- What resources you do have

You don't need to be good at math.

You don't need fancy software.

You just need honesty, a pen, and a place to begin.

Step One – Financial Triage

This is your emergency financial response plan. Before you try to "fix" anything, just name what's essential.

Must Pay To Survive

Write down your current costs in each essential category:

Category	Monthly Cost	Due Date & Notes
Rent / Mortgage		
Food / Groceries		
Utilities (Gas, Elec.)		
Transportation		
Childcare (if needed)		

Can Delay or Reduce

These are things you may be able to postpone, pause, or negotiate.

Category	Monthly Cost	Action Step (Pause? Reduce?)
Subscriptions		
Credit Card Payments		
Gym Membership		
Streaming Services		

Can Cut (At Least for Now)

Extras you can trim for a season while you stabilize.

Category	Monthly Cost	Action Step (Pause? Reduce?)
Takeout / Delivery		
Gifts		
Non-Essential Shopping		
Delivery Fees / Apps		

Financial Triage Summary Tool

Below, list all current bills and expenses you can think of. Then, check the box that fits the category. Keep going until you've named every recurring cost you can.

Expense	Amount	Due Date	Must Pay	Can Delay	Cut
			☐	☐	☐
			☐	☐	☐
			☐	☐	☐
			☐	☐	☐
			☐	☐	☐
			☐	☐	☐
			☐	☐	☐
			☐	☐	☐
			☐	☐	☐
			☐	☐	☐
			☐	☐	☐
			☐	☐	☐
			☐	☐	☐
			☐	☐	☐
			☐	☐	☐
			☐	☐	☐

Your Next Steps:

- Highlight any due dates coming up within the next 2 weeks

- Mark anything you can pause or cancel today

- Set a reminder to revisit this list weekly for updates

Find the Experts you need at freshstartsregistry.com/experts

Monthly Income Tracker

Includes recurring and irregular sources of money with space to update weekly.

List Your Income Sources

Income Source	Amount	Frequency (Weekly, Monthly, One-time)	Notes / Date Received
Child support / Spousal support (if applicable)			
SNAP / Government benefits			
Loan or gift from friend/family			
Side gig or freelance work			
Cash savings used this month			
Refunds / Rebates / Credits			

Weekly Update Section

Use this space to jot down anything new that comes in during the month. Update as often as you can—even small updates matter.

	Income Received ($)	Source	Notes
Week 1			
Week 2			
Week 3			
Week 4			

Tips:

- Be honest, not idealistic—this tracker is here to help, not judge

- Keep this list somewhere easy to access (folder, notes app, printed worksheet)

- Add any future expected income—even if it's just $20 from a friend for helping them move

- Update weekly so you can start to see patterns, gaps, and possibilities

Where Your Money Is Going (and What You Can Do About It)

Now that you know what's coming in, let's get clear about what's going out.

Use a blank piece of paper or our worksheet to list:

- Your current bills

- Minimum payments

- Food costs (weekly average)

- Gas or public transportation

- Any known upcoming expenses (court filings, school supplies, etc.)

Then look for one small change you can make this week. That's it. You don't need to gut your life—just shift one lever.

Free Tools That Can Help

You don't need to spend money to track money. These apps and services are free, beginner-friendly, and don't require linking your bank account (unless you want to).

Recommended tools:

- Goodbudget: Envelope-style budgeting for beginners

- EveryDollar (free version): Simple and visual

- Google Sheets or Excel: Use our pre-made template!

- Paper + pen: Still counts!

- Fresh Starts Simple Google Sheets Budget Template (fsr.pub/budget)

Budget-Friendly Food Shopping & Meal Planning

Feed Your Family Without Losing Your Mind (or Your Wallet)

When you're trying to feed kids on a tight budget—especially when you're going through a divorce and maybe dealing with SNAP applications, legal fees, or irregular income—it can feel impossible to make meals work. You are not failing. Food insecurity is real, and the system often makes it harder than it should be.

This section isn't about Pinterest-perfect meal plans. It's about getting food on the table that's comforting, realistic, and doable with limited time, energy, and cash. You deserve to feel proud of what you're pulling together. This is real-life nourishment, not performance.

Budget Builder Worksheet

This worksheet is designed for households navigating:

- No income
- Part-time or freelance income
- Shifting support situations (court, custody, etc.)
- High unpredictability

Tip: Don't aim for perfection. Aim for visibility. The goal is to see it so you can respond to it.

Where Your Money Is Going (and What You Can Do About It)

Now that you know what's coming in, let's get clear on what's going out.

This worksheet helps you lay it all out in one place—without shame or overwhelm. Just clarity. You don't need to gut your life. You just need to shift one lever at a time. Start here.

Your Current Monthly Expenses: Fill in what you currently spend or owe—ballpark is okay!

Expense Category	Amount	Notes (Due Dates, Flexibility, Priority)
Rent / Mortgage		
Electricity / Gas / Water		
Internet / Cell Phone		
Groceries (weekly x 4)		
Transportation (gas, metro, etc.)		
Minimum Credit Card Payments		
Loan Payments (auto, student)		
Childcare		
Medical / Prescription Costs		
Insurance (health, auto, home)		
Streaming / Subscriptions		
Other Monthly Bills		
TOTAL MONTHLY EXPENSES		

Known or Upcoming Expenses: These are one-time or seasonal costs you know are coming up soon.

Upcoming Expense (What & When)	Estimated Cost	Notes / Deadline

One Small Shift You Can Make This Week: What's one change you can make to lighten your load?

☐ Cancel or pause a subscription?

☐ Cook at home once more this week?

☐ Use public transit once instead of driving?

☐ Call a provider to ask for a payment extension or plan?

This week, I will: _____

_____

_____

Grocery Shopping Tips on a Budget

Plan for 2–3 main meals and repeat them. Kids don't need variety—they need familiarity. Rotating favorites saves money and energy.

Stick to flexible ingredients. Think: rice, beans, pasta, eggs, canned tomatoes, frozen veggies, tortillas, potatoes, oats, and peanut butter.

Buy store-brand everything. It's often identical to name brand but 30–50% cheaper.

Frozen over fresh. Frozen produce is just as nutritious, lasts longer, and reduces waste.

Use price-matching apps. Tools like Flipp, Basket, or your store's own app can help compare prices.

Use SNAP, WIC, food pantries, or mutual aid. These resources are for exactly this situation. You are not taking from others—you are the person they exist to support.

A Week of Budget Meals

(Designed for One Parent + 2–3 Kids)

This meal plan uses overlapping ingredients, requires minimal prep, and includes options for picky eaters. Adjust for allergies, preferences, or whatever's in your pantry.

MONDAY

Breakfast: Peanut butter on toast + banana

Lunch: Turkey and cheese roll-ups + carrot sticks + pretzels

Dinner: Pasta with jarred sauce + frozen peas + garlic toast (from sandwich bread)

TUESDAY

Breakfast: Oatmeal with brown sugar + apples

Lunch: Quesadillas (cheese + canned beans in tortillas) + apple slices

Dinner: Baked potatoes with shredded cheese, broccoli, and optional canned chili

WEDNESDAY

Breakfast: Cereal + milk

Lunch: Hummus and crackers + cucumber rounds + grapes

Dinner: Stir-fried frozen veggies and rice with scrambled eggs or tofu

THURSDAY

Breakfast: Yogurt with oats and fruit

Lunch: DIY lunchables: crackers, sliced cheese, lunch meat, cucumber slices

Dinner: Slow cooker soup: lentils, carrots, canned tomatoes, broth (or bouillon)

FRIDAY

Breakfast: Toast with butter and jam + hard-boiled egg

Lunch: Pasta salad with frozen veggies + ranch or vinaigrette

Dinner: Make-your-own tacos with ground beef or beans, lettuce, cheese, salsa

SATURDAY

Breakfast: Oatmeal or cereal

Lunch: PB&J sandwiches + baby carrots + goldfish or popcorn

Dinner: Breakfast for dinner: scrambled eggs, pancakes, and fruit

SUNDAY

Breakfast: Leftovers or cereal

Lunch: Grilled cheese + tomato soup (canned or from scratch)

Dinner: "Clean out the fridge" night: leftovers, snack plates, or sandwiches

Pantry Meal Life-Savers (Always Good to Have On Hand)

- Pasta + jarred sauce
- Canned beans + tortillas = instant burritos
- Boxed mac & cheese + frozen peas
- Rice + egg + soy sauce
- Peanut butter + crackers or apples
- Instant oats + raisins + cinnamon
- Frozen veggies + any protein + starch = balanced bowl

Budgeting Without Shame

You might feel embarrassed, anxious, or triggered looking at these numbers. That's normal. If you've never been allowed or encouraged to manage money, this might feel like stepping into a brand-new identity.

But here's what we want you to remember:

- You are not irresponsible—you were unpaid.
- You are not behind—you are starting now.
- Budgeting is not about restriction—it's about freedom.

Give yourself a break. You don't have to "do money" perfectly. You just have to keep looking at it, even when it's hard.

This chapter isn't about fixing your finances overnight. It's about proving to yourself that you can face your numbers—and you can make them work for you.

Let's keep going.

CHAPTER 8

———

Applying for Benefits + Emergency Resources

This chapter is for anyone who's ever said, "I can't afford to get divorced." If you're a stay-at-home parent with no income—or no control over the income—you may qualify for government help. These programs exist because people like you exist. There is no shame in using the systems that are meant to protect families during hard times. Whether you need food, healthcare, housing, cash assistance, or all of the above, we're going to show you exactly where to go and what to do—step by step.

First, What You Might Qualify For

Let's break down the most common emergency and long-term public assistance programs that can help stay-at-home parents during divorce:

SNAP (Supplemental Nutrition Assistance Program)

- Formerly known as "food stamps"
- Provides monthly funds for groceries
- Comes on an EBT card (works like a debit card)
- Based on household income and number of dependents

WIC (Women, Infants & Children)

- Offers nutrition support for pregnant/postpartum parents and children under 5
- Covers formula, healthy groceries, and nutrition education

Medicaid / CHIP

- Free or low-cost healthcare coverage
- Medicaid covers adults and children (especially if you've lost insurance from a spouse)
- CHIP covers children if your income is slightly too high for Medicaid

TANF (Temporary Assistance for Needy Families)

- Monthly cash support (can be used for rent, bills, or other needs)
- Comes with work or job-readiness requirements (these may be waived depending on your situation)

Housing Assistance

- Vouchers, public housing, or emergency shelter resources
- Includes programs through HUD, local nonprofits, and DV agencies

Emergency Aid from Local Organizations

- Food pantries, diaper banks, back-to-school drives, gas vouchers, and eviction prevention grants
- Often available faster than federal or state aid

How to Apply for SNAP, WIC, and Medicaid

Step 1: Find Your State's Application Website

Search:

> "[Your state] SNAP application"
>
> "[Your state] Medicaid application"
>
> "[Your state] WIC clinic near me"
>
> Each state has its own portal—some allow you to apply for multiple benefits at once.

Step 2: Gather Your Documents

You may be asked for:

- Photo ID

- Proof of income (or a signed statement saying you have no income)

- Social Security numbers for you and your children

- Proof of address (a lease, utility bill, or official mail)

- School enrollment for your children (optional but helpful)

- If you don't have these, still apply. You can usually submit missing documents later.

Step 3: Make the Call or Apply Online

Many states allow you to apply over the phone or through a website. You may have to do a follow-up interview by phone.

Sample Script:

"Hi, I'm a stay-at-home parent currently going through a divorce. I don't have income right now, but I need help with groceries and health insurance for my children. Can you help me figure out how to apply for SNAP and Medicaid?"

What to Do If You're at Risk of Losing Housing

If you're being pressured to leave your home, facing eviction, or don't have anywhere to go, here are your options:

- Contact Local Housing Support Programs

- Call 211 or visit 211.org to find local housing help

- Search "[Your city] housing assistance" or "[Your county] family shelter services"

- Ask for rapid rehousing, transitional housing, or rental assistance options

Domestic Violence Agencies

Even if you aren't being physically hurt, many DV organizations help people facing coercion, isolation, or financial abuse.

They can help with:

- Emergency shelter
- Transportation
- Relocation funds
- Legal support
- Protective orders (if needed)

DV shelters often have family rooms and caseworkers to help you stabilize quickly.

How to Ask for Help Without Shame

If you've never applied for benefits before, it's normal to feel nervous, embarrassed, or afraid of being judged. But here's what you need to know:

- These programs exist because people like you exist.
- You are not "taking" from the system—you're using it as intended.
- Needing help during a life transition is not a failure. It's survival.

If the application feels confusing or overwhelming, ask someone to sit with you while you do it. A friend, a school social worker, a legal aid assistant. You don't have to do it alone.

What Happens After You Apply

Depending on the program, you may:

- Get a call for a phone interview (within 7–10 days)
- Be asked for additional documents
- Receive a benefits approval notice in the mail
- Get an EBT or Medicaid card within 2–4 weeks

If you're denied, don't panic. You can reapply, appeal, or ask a local legal clinic for help. Many denials are fixable.

Emergency Resources You Can Use Today

You don't have to wait for government systems to process your application to get help. These resources are often available same-day:

- Local food pantries (many are open weekly—no ID required)

- Diaper banks and formula drives (ask at WIC or 211)

- School districts—free lunch, hygiene kits, and mental health help

- Libraries—internet access, printing, free activity kits for kids, often have little pantries

- Mutual aid groups in your city (search Facebook or Reddit)

You are not broken. You are not failing. You are navigating one of the hardest systems in the world with grit, heart, and courage. And there is help out there—you deserve every bit of it.

CHAPTER 9

Making Money
(Even in Tiny Amounts)

One of the scariest questions you face as a stay-at-home parent navigating divorce is: "How will I earn money?" If you've been out of the workforce—or never formally entered it—this chapter is your re-entry ramp. You don't need to land a full-time job tomorrow. You just need to begin. Whether that means a few hours of flexible work, trading skills with neighbors, or slowly building income while parenting solo, we'll walk you through how to start earning again—on your terms.

Starting Where You Are

Let's begin by letting go of the idea that you need to "get back to work" in a big way to make money. You are already working—unpaid parenting labor is real. Now we're going to help you find ways to translate those skills into income, even if:

- You have no childcare

- You're burned out

- You haven't had a paycheck in a decade

- You don't have a resume (yet)

- You're not behind. You're building forward.

What Can You Offer—Right Now?

Let's talk about transferable skills—the kind you already use every day that people will pay for.

Ask yourself:

- What do people already come to me for help with?

- What do I enjoy doing that I could offer for pay?

- What needs exist in my community that I could fill?

- What would I do for $20 today if I really had to?

Examples of Parent-to-Income Skills:

- Meal prep → sell freezer meals or snacks

- Childcare → babysit, be a mother's helper, offer evening care

- Organizing → help friends with closets, paperwork, moving

- Communication → write resumes, edit papers, tutor reading

- Emotional labor → virtual assistant, scheduling, customer support

Transferable Skills Brainstorm Worksheet

What Can You Offer—Right Now?

You don't need a new degree or a full-time job to start earning. You just need to recognize the skills you already use every day—the ones people would gladly pay for. This worksheet will help you brainstorm realistic, doable income ideas using your transferable skills.

Start Here: Ask Yourself

Take a few moments to reflect and jot down your honest answers.

Prompt	Answer
What do people already come to me for help with?	
What do I enjoy doing that I could offer for pay?	
What needs exist in my community (or online) that I could fill?	
If I had to earn $20 today, what would I do right now?	

Examples of Parent-to-Income Skills

These are everyday actions that become income streams with just a little intention:

Skill You Already Use	Potential Income Idea	Can You Do This Now? (Yes / Maybe / No)
Meal prep	Sell freezer meals, snacks, or baked goods	
Childcare	Babysit, offer evening care, mother's helper	
Organizing	Declutter closets, sort paperwork, help with moves	
Communication	Write resumes, tutor, edit or proofread	
Emotional labor / Planning	Virtual assistant, customer support, scheduling	

Brainstorm: Your Transferable Skills Inventory

List out all your everyday superpowers—don't filter! Think about parenting, volunteering, home management, emotional labor, and hobbies.

I'm good at...	How someone might pay me to do this

Next Step: Choose One to Explore

Pick one idea to try or learn more about this week:

Idea I want to explore: _____

One small action I can take this week: _____

Small Ways to Start Making Money Fast

You do not need a business plan or career path right now. You need a cash trickle. Here are realistic, flexible ways to start earning, even with limited hours or support:

Local, In-Person Income Ideas

- Babysitting during evenings or weekends

- Pet sitting or dog walking

- Selling baked goods, handmade crafts, or gently used items

- House cleaning or organizing for neighbors

- Running errands or driving elderly neighbors to appointments

Online, Remote-Friendly Ideas

- Virtual assistant (email, calendar, data entry)

- Customer service (many companies hire part-time remote)

- Freelance writing or editing (Upwork, Fiverr, Freelancer)

- Transcription (Rev.com, Scribie)

- Tutoring (reading, ESL, test prep)

Rebuilding Your Resume + Work Confidence

Even if your last job title was "Snack Fetcher-in-Chief," you have experience that matters.

Let's build a resume that reflects that:

- Start with a functional resume that highlights skills, not gaps

- Use language like "Household Manager" or "Primary Caregiver" with clear tasks and accomplishments

- Include any volunteer work, community organizing, or informal side work

- Create a free resume on Canva

Sample Entry:

Primary Caregiver | Household CEO | 2016–Present
Managed complex family scheduling, budgeting, and logistics
Coordinated all school, healthcare, and developmental needs for two children
Maintained household systems and supported child development with educational activities

Find the Experts you need at freshstartsregistry.com/experts

Rebuilding Your Resume + Work Confidence

Even if your last official title was "Snack Fetcher-in-Chief," you've been doing real work—managing, planning, organizing, supporting, adapting.

Let's build a resume that reflects the truth: You are experienced, capable, and hireable.

Start With a Functional Resume Format

This style focuses on skills and accomplishments, not chronological gaps.

- Highlight key skills at the top
- Use strong, clear language for caregiving roles
- Group experience by function (ex: project management, communication, scheduling)
- Include informal work, volunteering, and community roles
- Create your resume for free at canva.com

Brainstorm Your Core Skills

Fill in what you're already doing every day that showcases your strengths:

Skill Area	Real-Life Examples You've Done
Organization	(e.g. managed school calendar, family logistics)
Communication	(e.g. emailed teachers/doctors, mediated sibling fights)
Budgeting	(e.g. grocery shopping, stretching a one-income budget)
Problem-Solving	(e.g. handling last-minute changes calmly)
Teaching / Coaching	(e.g. helped with homework, taught life skills)
Tech Savvy	(e.g. ran Zooms, managed family apps & devices)

Build Your Resume

Start here with a template:

> Primary Caregiver | Household CEO
>
> City, State | [Years, e.g. 2016–Present]
>
> Managed complex scheduling, transportation, and appointments for family
>
> Oversaw household budget, purchasing, and planning
>
> Coordinated healthcare, school communications, and daily routines
>
> Developed and implemented systems for home organization and child development
>
> Navigated high-stress, multitasking environments with empathy and efficiency

Language Bank: Resume-Ready Words

Swap "mom stuff" for resume gold:

Real-Life Task	Resume Language
Made lunches, did school drop-offs	Coordinated daily logistics and routines
Paid bills, handled groceries	Managed household budget and procurement
Ran the PTA bake sale	Led volunteer-based fundraising efforts
Advocated at IEP meetings	Navigated educational systems and supports
Mediated tantrums	Resolved conflicts with emotional intelligence
Took care of everything	Oversaw full-time household operations

Add Volunteer & Informal Work

Don't skip this—it counts:

Real-Life Task	Resume Language
Ran social media for church/school group	Digital marketing, content creation
Helped friend declutter and move	Organizing, project management
Volunteered at local food pantry	Inventory tracking, team coordination
Co-led parenting group	Community building, facilitation

Next Steps:

- Pick a free Canva resume template that feels modern and clean
- Use your brainstormed language and copy/paste it into your draft
- Keep it to 1 page if possible, and lead with your skills and wins
- Add confidence as you go—you've done more than you realize

Find the Experts you need at freshstartsregistry.com/experts

Sample Resume:

JANE DOE [Your City, State] jane.doe@email.com | (123) 456-7890 | LinkedIn.com/in/janedoe

PROFESSIONAL SUMMARY

Adaptable, resourceful, and results-driven professional re-entering the workforce after dedicating several years to full-time parenting. Proven ability to lead with empathy, manage complex logistics, and handle high-stakes decision-making under pressure. Ready to bring strong communication, multitasking, and problem-solving skills to a mission-driven team. Eager to contribute fresh energy, creative thinking, and a relentless work ethic honed through years of running a household, supporting a family, and staying actively engaged in community, learning, and growth.

CORE SKILLS & STRENGTHS

- Project and time management
- Budgeting and financial oversight
- Conflict resolution and mediation
- Crisis management and adaptability
- Event planning and scheduling
- Clear and compassionate communication
- Leadership and team coordination
- Creative problem-solving
- Emotional intelligence and empathy
- Digital literacy (Google Workspace, Microsoft Office, social media platforms)

PROFESSIONAL EXPERIENCE

Chief Household Officer — Full-Time Parent 2017–2024

Led a dynamic, multi-person operation focused on growth, education, and well-being. Managed daily logistics, long-term planning, and high-pressure decision-making with strategy and heart.

- Directed budgeting, purchasing, and resource allocation with efficiency and frugality
- Developed and maintained complex schedules across multiple stakeholders
- Navigated high-emotion situations with diplomacy and emotional intelligence
- Led volunteer efforts, classroom support, and extracurricular coordination
- Learned new systems and adapted rapidly in changing environments (e.g., remote learning)
- Maintained a continuous learning mindset, pursuing personal and professional development

Freelance Consultant / Community Volunteer | Various Organizations, Ongoing

- Served as PTO member, classroom coordinator, and event planner for school programs
- Volunteered with [Organization Name] to support [brief description]
- Provided informal consulting and peer support in areas of parenting, education, and life transitions
- Managed social media accounts and newsletters for local nonprofits

PRIOR WORK EXPERIENCE

Marketing Coordinator - XYZ Company | New York, NY | 2012–2016

- Supported integrated marketing campaigns, collaborated across departments, and tracked performance
- Wrote and edited content for internal and external communications
- Managed scheduling and logistics for product launches and team events

EDUCATION

B.A. in Communications, University of Anywhere | Graduated 2011

PROFESSIONAL DEVELOPMENT & TRAINING

- Google Workspace Certification (In Progress)
- Conflict Resolution & Nonviolent Communication (Community Workshop, 2023)
- LinkedIn Learning: Project Management Foundations (2024)

Where to Find Low-Stakes Jobs That Work for You

You don't have to apply for 40 jobs a week to get moving. Here's where to find flexible, low-barrier roles:

Online

- Facebook groups (search your town's moms group, yard sale, or babysitting board)

- Care.com (for babysitting, pet care, senior care)

- Remote job boards: Working Nomads, The Mom Project, FlexJobs (some listings are free), Upwork/Fiverr for project-based freelance gigs, Hire My Mom, Dreamers and Doers, Harlow, and Mother Untitled

Local

- Bulletin boards at libraries, schools, churches

- Ask around at your kids' school or daycare

- Community centers and job readiness nonprofits

Managing Your Energy + Time

Solo parenting + starting over + emotional recovery = you don't have endless hours or bandwidth. That's okay.

Here are tips to make work fit your life:

- Start with "micro-jobs" (30 mins–2 hours)

- Build "focus hours" into your week (even if it's just one)

- Set boundaries with clients (working hours, response time)

- Say no to anything that burns you out faster than it pays

You are allowed to:

- Work slowly

- Take breaks

- Be proud of any income

You don't need to rebuild your financial life overnight. You just need to earn your first $20, then your next. And you'll get there. One tiny, powerful, badass step at a time.

CHAPTER 10

Building a Divorce Support Team

Divorce is hard. Doing it alone is even harder. But here's the good news: you don't have to do it alone. In this chapter, we'll show you how to build your personal divorce support team—a mix of professionals, helpers, and emotional allies who will hold your hand, answer your questions, and walk with you as you rebuild. Whether you have $0 or $1000, whether you're just thinking about divorce or knee-deep in paperwork, this chapter will help you figure out who to bring in— and where to find help that fits your budget and your needs.

And if you're looking for deeper guidance on exactly why you need these experts, how to interview them, and what to ask before you hire anyone, check out another book in the Divorce Guide Series: Your Divorce Support Team: 250+ Questions to Help You Build Your Divorce Support Team. It's your go-to guide for navigating divorce with clarity and confidence—packed with expert insights and over 250 essential questions to protect your finances, advocate for your emotional well-being, and assemble the support you deserve. You can download the ebook or PDF for free at FreshStartsRegistry.com, or snag a hard copy wherever books are sold.

What Is a Divorce Support Team?

Your divorce support team is the group of people who will help you make legal, emotional, logistical, and financial decisions during this process.

You do not need to hire a high-powered divorce lawyer to have a team. Your team might include:

- A lawyer, mediator, or legal aid rep
- A financial coach or advisor
- A therapist or trauma-informed coach
- A parent coach or co-parenting expert
- A friend who helps you stay grounded
- A nonprofit advocate who helps with benefits or housing
- An organizer to help with your space, your stuff, or your paperwork

Some of these people you may pay. Some will be free. Some will be chosen. Some will just show up. Your team = your power circle.

What do all these people do?

A lawyer, mediator, or legal aid rep: These are the people who help you understand and handle the legal side of divorce. A lawyer can represent you in court. A mediator helps both people talk things through and make fair decisions together. A legal aid rep helps people who may not be able to afford a lawyer get legal support.

A financial coach or advisor: This person helps you understand your money. They can help you make a budget, plan for the future, and feel more in control of your finances during and after the divorce.

A therapist or trauma-informed coach: They're here to support your heart and mind. They help you work through your feelings, understand your reactions, and heal from anything painful you're going through—especially if your divorce is bringing up past hurts.

A parent coach or co-parenting expert: This person helps you figure out how to parent through a divorce. They can support you with things like setting routines, talking to your kids about what's happening, or learning how to co-parent peacefully with your ex.

A friend who helps you stay grounded: This is your person who listens without judgment, brings you snacks, and reminds you who you are when everything feels like too much. You don't have to go through this alone—and this friend helps you remember that.

A nonprofit advocate who helps with benefits or housing: This person works with a nonprofit and helps you find support like food assistance, safe housing, childcare help, or other benefits you may be eligible for. They know the systems and help you navigate them.

An organizer to help with your space, your stuff, or your paperwork: This person helps bring order to the chaos. Whether it's sorting through your closet, packing up boxes, or organizing your important papers, they help make your space calmer and your to-do list less stressful.

Who Do You Actually Need?

Not everyone needs a full legal dream team. Start with the basics and build from there, based on your specific situation.

Legal

- Lawyer (paid or legal aid) if your divorce is contested or your safety is at risk

- Mediator if you're separating amicably and need help creating agreements

- Court navigator or legal advocate to help explain the steps in your state

Financial

- Financial coach to help you budget and plan post-divorce

- Certified Divorce Financial Analyst (CDFA) if you have property, retirement, or alimony questions

- Benefits navigator to help with SNAP, housing, and Medicaid

Emotional + Mental Health

- Therapist who understands divorce, family systems, and trauma

- Divorce coach who can help with mindset, confidence, and step-by-step guidance

- Support group (online or in-person) to stay connected and validated

Parenting + Co-Parenting

- Co-parenting coach to help you build a plan that puts your kids first

- Parenting coordinator if conflict is high

- School counselor or social worker as a built-in support for your kids

Where to Find the Right People (Without Breaking the Bank)

You don't need to start Googling and hoping for the best. The world of divorce help is noisy—and not all of it's safe, ethical, or affordable.

Start with Fresh Starts Registry

At Fresh Starts, we've built the world's leading vetted expert directory for people going through major life transitions—especially divorce. Every expert in our network is personally vetted, values-aligned, and trauma-informed. You can:

- Browse all expert categories (legal, financial, mental health, home, parenting, and more)

- Search by state or specialty

- Book directly from their profiles

- Visit: www.freshstartsregistry.com/experts

- Browse anytime. No payment or login required.

Get Free 1:1 Help with a Divorce Resource Consultation

Not sure what you need? We've got you.

You can book a free, private, no-judgment divorce resource consultation with Olivia Howell, co-founder of Fresh Starts Registry and certified life, success, and divorce coach. Olivia will:

- Listen to your story

- Help you identify your top 2–3 needs

- Match you with vetted, aligned professionals

- Recommend free and low-cost next steps

- Offer emotional support and practical clarity

It's completely free. There's no upsell. Just support.

Book a free consult here: www.freshstartsregistry.com/consult

How to Know If Someone Is a Good Fit

Whether it's a lawyer, coach, or therapist, here are green flags to look for:

- They listen more than they lecture

- They use trauma-informed or inclusive language

- They're upfront about pricing and scope

- They don't make you feel rushed or ashamed

- They honor your parenting experience—even if it wasn't paid

And red flags?

- Pressure to sign a contract right away

- Overpromising (ex: "We'll get you everything!")

- Dismissing your lived experience

- Not transparent about pricing or policies

Build a Team That Feels Like Safety

Your support team should never feel like one more thing to manage. They should feel like:

- A deep exhale

- A steady hand

- A no-bullshit friend who says, "Let's figure this out."

You don't need ten experts. You don't need to do it all now. But you do deserve a circle of people who see you, hear you, and support your healing and your goals. Even if it's just one person to start.

You don't have to be the only one holding this. Support is not a luxury—it's a necessity. And now, it's within reach. Let's keep going.

CHAPTER 11

Opening Your Own Accounts + Collecting Documents

Let's be clear: this chapter isn't about confrontation—it's about protection.

Before you file a single piece of paper or share a single plan with your spouse, it's time to quietly set the foundation beneath your feet. That doesn't mean blowing up your life overnight—it means starting to build the financial and legal infrastructure that will support your next chapter, even if no one else knows you're doing it yet.

Think of this like packing a go-bag, but for your future. It's calm. It's careful. And it's entirely within your control.

Whether you're still under the same roof or already living apart, these small, strategic steps will help you begin creating a sense of safety, sovereignty, and stability. This is your first quiet claim to space. It's not about being sneaky—it's about being smart. It's about ensuring that when the time comes to take a bigger leap, you've already laid the bricks behind the scenes.

You don't need to know everything right now. You don't need a perfect plan. You don't even need confidence—you just need to move forward with care. A few folders. A safe place for your documents. A clear idea of what's yours and what's not.

This is your start. This is your power.

Let's begin.

Why Opening Your Own Bank Account Matters

If you've never had a bank account in your own name—or you've been relying on joint funds—it's time to start creating financial separation.

Even if you're not earning income yet, having a personal account allows you to:

- Apply for benefits like SNAP or Medicaid

- Cash checks or receive Venmo/Zelle payments

- Start saving any small amounts that come your way

- Protect what is yours

Note: Opening a personal account doesn't mean you're hiding money—it means you're safeguarding yourself.

How to Open a Personal Bank Account (Even If You Have No Income)

What you'll usually need:

- A government-issued photo ID (driver's license, passport, etc.)

- Social Security number or ITIN

- Proof of address (utility bill, lease, or mail from a government agency)

- Sometimes an opening deposit (many banks accept $25 or less)

Where to go:

Credit unions and community banks are often more flexible than big banks

Some online banks like Chime, Capital One 360, SoFi, or Ally allow $0 minimums and are easy to open digitally

Sample script for the bank: "Hi, I'm opening a personal account for the first time and want to make sure I bring everything I need. I'm a stay-at-home parent and don't currently have income—can you help me get started?"

Documents to Collect (and How to Store Them Safely)

In divorce, paper is power. You'll need certain documents for court, custody, benefits applications, and long-term stability. Even if you don't know what to do with them yet, collecting them now will make things much easier down the road.

Identity + Family

- Your driver's license or state ID
- Marriage certificate
- Your children's birth certificates
- Social Security cards (yours + kids')
- Passport(s)

Financial

- Bank statements (shared or solo)
- Credit card statements
- Tax returns (2–3 years)
- Pay stubs (if applicable)
- Proof of benefits (SNAP, WIC, Medicaid)
- Loan or mortgage statements

Legal

- Prenuptial or postnuptial agreements
- Court orders (existing custody, restraining orders, etc.)
- Leases or property deeds
- Insurance policies

Find the Experts you need at freshstartsregistry.com/experts

Divorce Documents Master List

In divorce, paper is power.

Even if you're not sure what to do with these documents yet, collecting them now will make court filings, custody discussions, benefits applications, and financial planning so much easier later.

Use this checklist to track what you've gathered, what's still missing, and where everything lives (folder, cloud, email, etc.).

dentity + Family Documents

Document	Have It	Need It	Where It's Stored
Your driver's license or state ID	☐	☐	
Marriage certificate	☐	☐	
Children's birth certificates	☐	☐	
Social Security cards (yours + kids)	☐	☐	
Passport(s)	☐	☐	

Legal & Housing Documents

Document	Have It	Need It	Where It's Stored
Prenuptial or postnuptial agreement (if any)	☐	☐	
Court orders (custody, restraining orders, etc)	☐	☐	
Lease or property deed(s)	☐	☐	
Insurance policies (health, auto, home, life)	☐	☐	

Legal & Housing Documents

Document	Have It	Need It	Where It's Stored
Prenuptial or postnuptial agreement (if any)	☐	☐	
Court orders (custody, restraining orders, etc)	☐	☐	
Lease or property deed(s)	☐	☐	
Insurance policies (health, auto, home, life)	☐	☐	

Tips for Using This Tool:

- Create both digital (Google Drive, Dropbox) and physical (binder or folder) copies

- Label each document clearly by type and date

- If you don't have access to a document, note who to ask or where to request it

- Check off items as you collect them—you're building power, piece by piece

Find the Experts you need at freshstartsregistry.com/experts

If You're Still Living Together—How to Do This Quietly

You may not feel safe or comfortable telling your spouse that you're preparing for divorce. That's not just okay—it's incredibly normal. A lot of stay-at-home parents begin this process quietly, not because they're being secretive, but because they're protecting their emotional and physical safety, financial wellbeing, and ability to think clearly.

Starting quietly doesn't mean you're doing anything wrong.

It means you're building a foundation behind the scenes so that if and when you're ready to take the next step, you won't be starting from zero. It's not about deception—it's about preparation.

These first steps are small, smart, and completely within your rights. You're allowed to begin organizing and safeguarding your information without making any announcements. You're allowed to gather what you need to stand on your own, even if you're still sharing a home.

Here are a few simple ways to begin this process with care:

Tips for quiet preparation:

- Take photos of important documents (like tax returns, account statements, health insurance info, mortgage or lease paperwork) instead of removing them

- Email scanned files to a new, secure email account only you can access (don't use a shared family account)

- Store files digitally in a password-protected cloud folder (Google Drive, Dropbox, etc.) or with a trusted friend or sibling

- Open a new personal bank account and set statements to paperless

- Change your mailing address with the bank or other key accounts to a trusted person's home, a PO box, or use paperless options

- Start a simple log of expenses and purchases—this can help you understand the household finances and may be helpful later if you need to demonstrate financial need

If you're worried about retaliation or tracking:

- Use incognito/private browser windows

- Use public Wi-Fi (like a library or cafe) when doing financial research

- Avoid leaving printed paperwork visible in shared spaces

- How to Organize What You're Collecting

You don't need a complicated filing system. Just start grouping documents into categories:

- Identity + Family

- Financial + Bank

- Legal + Housing

- Health + Insurance

Create a simple spreadsheet or use a printable checklist to track what you've gathered and what's missing. You can keep everything in:

- A portable file box or expanding folder

- A password-protected USB drive

- A cloud folder labeled something neutral like "Paperwork 2024"

What to Do If You Can't Get the Documents

If your spouse controls the mail, the bank logins, or the tax files—you are not out of luck. Later in the divorce process, your lawyer (or the court) can request financial disclosure.

But for now:

- Make a list of what you know exists

- Write down names of banks, accounts, employers, and insurance companies

- Note details you've overheard or seen (e.g. "Retirement account with Fidelity")

- This kind of "shadow bookkeeping" can be incredibly helpful when it's time to file.

This isn't about confrontation. It's about quiet, steady protection. You are building a foundation—even if it's made of scanned PDFs and secret Google Drives right now. You're doing it.

CHAPTER 12

Planning for the Next Chapter

You've done so much hard, brave work already. You've said the words. You've made the calls. You've opened accounts and started budgeting. And maybe right now, things still feel messy. That's okay. This chapter isn't about tying everything up in a neat little bow. It's about asking yourself: What comes next, and how do I build it—my way?

Let's create a gentle rhythm for your new life, explore your long-term vision, and set up realistic goals that feel doable—not daunting. You don't need to become a whole new person. You just need to start becoming yourself again.

You're Not Starting Over from Nothing

You may feel like your life got bulldozed—but that's not the whole truth.

You're starting with:

- Deep knowledge of your children's needs

- Experience managing a household

- Emotional survival skills you never asked for, but learned anyway

- New boundaries, new courage, and new tools

- A commitment to do this life differently

This chapter is about taking those hard-won pieces and laying them down, one at a time, to rebuild your foundation.

Creating a New Weekly Rhythm

When you're parenting alone, healing, and possibly working part-time or navigating the court system, you need structure that supports you—not traps you.

Try this simple rhythm exercise:

- One anchor activity each day (ex: therapy Monday, laundry Tuesday, benefit office Wednesday, library Thursday)

- One meal you can count on

- One moment of rest, even if it's five minutes

Setting Small Goals That Actually Matter

Big goals can feel overwhelming. Let's shrink them down.

Use this framework:

- One-month goal → What do I want to feel or finish by next month?

- Three-month goal → What would help me feel more stable?

- Six-month goal → What do I want to reclaim, learn, or start building?

Examples:

- "Apply for Medicaid and have one appointment scheduled."

- "Rework my resume and apply to three jobs."

- "Set up a parenting plan and stick to it for one month."

- "Call a therapist and book a free consult."

"What I Want Next" – Reclaiming Your Vision

This is where you get to dream a little—not about being perfect, but about being free. No more running your life according to someone else's rules.

Prompt yourself:

- What does peace look like in my home?

- What kind of mornings do I want?

- What do I want my kids to remember about this time?

- What kind of people do I want around me now?

- What do I want to do with my one wild and precious next chapter?

Normalize the Hard Days

Even as you move forward, there will be hard days. That's not failure—that's being human. You may feel like you're doing great one morning and want to crawl into bed by afternoon.

That's okay. Remember: You are not doing this wrong. You are doing something hard.

Creating a Fresh Starts Divorce Registry

Just like people create baby or wedding registries to celebrate a new chapter, you deserve to be supported as you rebuild yours. A Fresh Starts Divorce Registry is a powerful, empowering way to ask for (and receive!) the practical and emotional tools you need to begin again. Whether you need pots and pans, new sheets, or a copy of your favorite book—you are worthy of help.

This isn't a luxury. It's a support system. And you don't need to justify it to anyone.

What Is a Divorce Registry?

A divorce registry is a curated list of the items you need to rebuild your home and your life after a separation. It's not about replacing everything all at once—it's about receiving meaningful, useful support as you start fresh.

The Fresh Starts Registry platform allows you to:

- Build a free, beautiful online registry
- Add any items you want (big, small, symbolic, practical)
- Write a personal note to explain your story (if you want)
- Share the link with friends, family, community, or followers
- Update or edit your registry anytime
- Receive items directly to your door

You can register for everything from bath towels to blenders to body butter. This is your fresh start.

What to Add to Your Registry

You don't have to justify needing a spatula, new pillows, or a soft robe. You're allowed to rebuild without shame.

Here are categories to consider:

- Home Essentials
- Dishes, cookware, utensils
- Cleaning supplies or small appliances
- Storage bins, laundry baskets
- Shower curtain, bath mats, towels

Comfort & Softness

- Sheets and bedding (especially if you left the marital bed)
- Pillows, throws, weighted blanket
- Robe, slippers, pajamas

Emotional Support

- Mugs, candles, affirmation decks
- Books that speak to your new chapter
- Journals, pens, self-care kits

Family & Kids

- Kid lunch supplies, bento boxes
- Water bottles, plasticware
- Snack bins, routine charts
- Board games or art supplies

Work & Rebuilding

- Laptop bag, desk lamp
- Headphones, printer, or organizers
- Resume paper or folders

How to Share Your Registry

Sharing your registry can feel vulnerable—but it's also brave. You're saying: I deserve support, too. And the truth is: people want to help. They just often don't know how.

You can share your registry link:

- In a personal text or email
- On social media with your story or a simple message
- In a community group or local parenting board
- With a trusted friend who can share on your behalf

Sample Message to Send:

"Hi friends—after going through a big life transition, I'm starting fresh and rebuilding my space for myself and my kids. I've put together a registry of a few things that would make this next chapter feel stable and comforting. If you're able to contribute or share, it means the world. Thank you for holding me up."

[Insert your registry link here]

How to Get Started

Building your registry is free, private, and super easy.

- Go to www.freshstartsregistry.com

- Click "Create Your Registry"

- Add items from any store—or browse curated suggestions

- Write a short note if you'd like

- Share when you're ready

There's no right or wrong way to do this. Whether your registry helps you replace what you left behind, or gives you a few new things that feel like yours—this is part of your healing.

You don't need to wait for permission to ask for help. You don't need to explain why you need a new pillow, or why receiving a $10 mug made you cry. You're not greedy. You're human. And this is a beautiful, bold step toward building a life that feels safe, stable, and fully yours.

You've done more than survive—you've started again. And no matter what happens next, you now have the tools to choose your path, one steady, sovereign step at a time. We're cheering for you. Every damn mile.

Resources we recommend:

Books for you:

Cooperative Co-Parenting for Secure Kids: The Attachment Theory Guide to Raising Kids in Two Homes by Aurisha Smolarski

Unhitched: The Essential Divorce Guide for Women by Oona Metz

No More Mediocre: A Call to Reimagine Our Relationships and Demand More by Laura Danger

Moms Moving On: Real-Life Advice on Conquering Divorce, Co-Parenting Through Conflict, and Becoming Your Best Self by by Michelle Dempsey-Multack

Better Divorce Blueprint: Workbook & Journal by Paulette Rigo

Divorce Decoded: A Manifesto for Women Navigating Divorce and Beyond by Donna Cates

Books for Kids:

The Invisible String by Patrice Karst

Divorce Is Not the End of the World: Zoe's and Evan's Coping Guide for Kids by Zoe and Evan Stern

Two Homes by Claire Masurel

Why Do Families Change?: Our First Talk About Separation and Divorce by Dr. Jillian Roberts

Standing on My Own Two Feet: A Child's Affirmation of Love in the Midst of Divorce by Tamara Schmitz

A Kids Book About Divorce by Ashley Simpo

The Family Book by Todd Parr

You Make Your Parents Super Happy by Richy K. Chandler

The Great Big Book of Families by Mary Hoffman

All About Families from Usborne Books

Who's in My Family? All About Our Families by Robie H. Harris

Fred Stays with Me by Nancy Coffelt

Children's Music About Divorce We Recommend:

The Fox and the Hare by The Okee Dokee Brothers, Brambletown

grown-up stuff by mama nous, change is inevitable

you are so easy to love by mama nous, change is inevitable

change is inevitable by mama nous, change is inevitable

Find the Experts you need at freshstartsregistry.com/experts

If You Are in an Unsafe or Controlling Relationship

If you've read this far and something in your gut is whispering "this isn't right," we want you to know: That voice inside you matters. You're not making it up. You're not being dramatic. You are allowed to want safety, dignity, and peace.

Even if no one ever hit you.

Even if you were told it's your fault.

Even if you have no money, no plan, or no proof.

Even if you're scared you won't be believed.

You will be. You are already believed here.

You don't need to call it abuse to reach out. If something in your relationship makes you feel afraid, trapped, powerless, or erased—you are allowed to ask for help.

What to Say When You Call a DV Hotline

You do not need to explain your entire situation. You do not need to have a perfect plan. You do not need to be calm or articulate.

You can just say:

"Hi, I'm not sure if this counts as abuse, but I don't feel safe in my relationship and I need someone to talk to."

"I'm a stay-at-home parent with no income, and I'm trying to figure out how to leave safely."

"I'm scared to even be making this call, but I don't know where else to turn. Can you help me talk through my options?"

Script for Chatting Online:

"I'm not in immediate danger, but I'm being controlled and financially cut off. I'm trying to leave. What resources are available?"

"My partner isn't violent, but I feel really unsafe emotionally and financially. I'm looking for help figuring out my next step."

U.S. Domestic Violence Resources (Free + Confidential)

National Domestic Violence Hotline

1-800-799-SAFE (7233)

Text "START" to 88788

www.thehotline.org

Available 24/7. Free. Confidential. Interpreters available.

StrongHearts Native Helpline

1-844-7NATIVE (1-844-762-8483)

www.strongheartshelpline.org

Culturally grounded support for Native American and Alaska Native communities.

WomensLaw.org

www.womenslaw.org

Includes legal info by state, and an anonymous Email a Lawyer feature.

Find Your Local Shelter or Advocacy Center

Search: "[Your County] + domestic violence services"

Or ask a hotline to help you locate safe housing and local advocates.

Many DV websites include a "quick exit" or "escape" button—clicking it will close the site and redirect you instantly. If you're worried about being tracked, use a library or friend's phone, or clear your browsing history.

A Note from Us

We know how scary it is to even consider that what you're living through isn't okay. But if something feels unsafe—it is unsafe. And you don't have to keep surviving alone.

Help exists. Plans exist. Soft landings do exist. You are allowed to reach for them.

You are worthy of care, safety, and support.

You are not too far gone.

You are not being dramatic.

You are allowed to leave.

And we are so, so proud of you.

You Did the Brave Thing

If you've made it to this page, we hope you know one thing above all else:

You are not alone.

You've done something incredibly brave. You faced a hard truth. You gathered information, asked hard questions, and opened doors that may have been locked for a long time. This journey isn't about perfection—it's about possibility. And you are already living proof that rebuilding is possible.

We wrote this book for people like you—stay-at-home parents who have spent years in caregiving roles, often with no income, limited resources, and a thousand worries about what comes next. You don't have to know everything. You just have to take the next small step. And then the next. And then the next.

You are already doing it.

Mantras to Carry With You

Say these aloud. Write them down. Keep them in your phone. They are truths, not wishes.

I am not selfish for wanting peace.

I am allowed to leave, even if things aren't "that bad."

I do not owe anyone my silence or my suffering.

I am allowed to need help and still be a strong, capable person.

I am not overreacting.

I deserve to be safe—in every way.

I can take up space in this world, with or without a partner.

I do not have to justify my pain to be worthy of healing.

I am not broken—I am rebuilding.

One Last Hug From Us

You've done something incredible. You've taken your power back, one small choice at a time. That matters. You matter.

We built Fresh Starts because we never want another woman—or any person—to go through this alone. If you need help, we're here. If you need someone to talk through your next step, you can always book a free consult with Olivia. There's no upsell, no judgment—just care.

We are so proud of you.

You are building a life that's rooted in truth, safety, and self-worth.

And we will be here, cheering you on, every brave mile.

With all our love,

Olivia & Jenny

Finding Support Through Fresh Starts Registry

At Fresh Starts Registry, we know that divorce is about more than paperwork. It's about rebuilding your life—emotionally, practically, and spiritually. That's why we've created a community-centered platform to walk with you through every step of your fresh start.

We offer tangible and emotional support for people navigating divorce and major life transitions. Whether you're still in the consideration phase or well into your new chapter, you don't have to do this alone.

What We Offer

The World's First Divorce Registry

You can create a registry of practical and supportive items—everything from bedsheets to books to blenders—so your friends and family can show up for you in meaningful ways. It's about celebrating your next chapter and giving you the tools to rebuild your home and life.

Expert Guidance and Referrals

We've built a trusted directory of vetted divorce professionals—from attorneys and therapists to financial advisors and real estate agents. These experts are here to support you with clarity and compassion. Need a personal referral? Reach out directly to our CEO, Olivia Howell, for a free support call.

Free Education and Resources

Our growing library of free e-books, guides, blog posts, and podcast episodes cover everything from parenting plans to financial prep to co-parenting etiquette. We believe education should be accessible—because knowledge is empowerment.

Community and Encouragement

Join our Instagram community @freshstartsregistry for daily support, real stories, and inspiration from people who have been exactly where you are. You'll also find updates on workshops, community events, and new resources.

Find the Experts you need at freshstartsregistry.com/experts

Get in Touch

Visit us at freshstartsregistry.com to explore the full platform.

Follow along on Instagram @freshstartsregistry

Email us anytime at hi@freshstartsregistry.com

You deserve support. You deserve celebration. You deserve a fresh start.

We're here to walk beside you.